D0393746

A GODLY HUMANISM

Francis Cardinal George, OMI

A GODLY HUMANISM

Clarifying the Hope That Lies Within

The Catholic University of America Press

Washington, D.C.

Copyright © 2015

Library of Congress Cataloging-in-Publication Data

George, Francis E. (Francis Eugene), 1937–2015.

[Essays. Selections]

Clarifying the hope that lies within / Cardinal Francis E. George.

pages cm

Includes bibliographical references and index.

ISBN 978-0-8132-2777-1 (cloth : alk. paper)

1. Catholic Church — Doctrines. 2. Catholics — United States —
Intellectual life — 20th century. 3. United States — Intellectual
life — 20th century. I. Title.

BX1751.3.G464 2015

230.2 — dc23   2015015958

Contents

Preface and Retrospective, vii

Acknowledgments, xiii

1. Saints in Catholic Intellectual Life   1

2. An Integrated Life   18

3. How God Thinks   45

4. A Christian Intellectual in a
   Post-Christian Society   76

5. A Christian Intellectual and
   the Moral Life   101

6. Education That Integrates
   Culture and Religion   129

7. Integrating the Second
   Vatican Council   145

8. Recent Popes and the Renewal
   of Catholic Intellectual Life   165

Bibliography, 193

Index, 199

Preface and Retrospective

THE ESSAYS IN THIS VOLUME are an exercise in integration. They are neither directly autobiographical nor straightforwardly historical, neither professionally theological nor distinctively spiritual in presentation, neither apologetic nor a thorough commentary on ecclesial life since the Second Vatican Council. They are useful, perhaps as markers along the way of a number of journeys, each of which I've made myself in various ways. I hope they are so considered because then they can be useful to others as aids to personal reflection, especially on the part of anyone who is striving to integrate wisdom and discipleship, which was the original title of the book.

As a Catholic and a bishop, I have worked to integrate my own thinking with that of the Church, God's instrument for handing on the most important truths about who he is and who we are. The papal Magisterium of the last fifty years, the years of my priestly life and ministry, has been developed in dialogue with the teachings of the Second Vatican Council, and each of the last several popes figures prominently in the final chapters of this book. Each, it seems to me as I explored his work, has brought a different emphasis to the interpretation of the Council's teaching and intention. If the Church is first of all a movement, built around a set of ideas, then political categories can be used to understand and interpret the Council, for ideas are either liberal or conservative. If, on the other hand, the Church is first of all a communion, as recent popes have insisted, then it is built around relationships, and we must begin not with ideas but with people in understanding it and integrating our lives within its horizon. Pope Paul VI responded to the Council's call to dialogue with the entire world. The vocation to dialogue brought him into conversation, in straightforward and direct manner, with the very poor and with those responsible for the present global economic order.

Pope John Paul II incorporated the Council's teaching on the human condition and introduced culture in strikingly novel ways as a privileged term of his papal Magisterium. For me, this was a providential turn, because it prompted me to study his theological and philosophical anthropology at the very moment when I was looking for tools to bring reflection on the relations between faith and culture into many conversations with missionaries around the world, each of whom opened up a new horizon of thinking and acting for me as I listened and watched them try to integrate faith and culture in preaching the Gospel to peoples who did not yet know who Jesus Christ is. Pope John Paul's teaching has contributed much to shaping my intellectual and spiritual life.

For me, Pope Benedict XVI's seamless incorporation of the Church fathers into the fullness of Catholic reflection was always moving, and he also brought me, for the first time in a serious manner, into internal dialogue with St. Bonaventure's intellectual and spiritual synthesis.

Now with Pope Francis, the Magisterium has taken on a unique presentation. He teaches through gestures, which are telling and of universal significance. They are, however, more easily open to different interpretations than are words; they evoke rather than define. His papal Magisterium is clearly rooted in ministry, with a primary concern for the poor, the first citizens of the Kingdom of heaven. His homilies are filled with the advice of a spiritual father who is very close to the faithful and who trusts the witness of their faith. His own witness is deeply marked by the freedom given him by the Holy Spirit working in his life. If this book were to be published a year from now, the incorporation of Pope Francis's Magisterium would be evidence of another horizon having been opened more clearly for believers.

The sequence of argument or development of the book can be seen in the use I make of each document, person, and event and the way in which interrelationships are traced among them. Since faith is creative of various ways of life, a vocation to the intellectual life as such must be a call for some within the faith community. When I was in high school, one of my teachers, an Oblate priest, recommended that I read *La Vie Intellectuelle*, by Antonin-Gilbert Sertillanges, OP. Unlike other books I had read, it didn't just report on something or offer explanations; rather, it opened up a vista, a horizon I would not have made explicit so early in my life without the help of the book and the advice of my teacher and elder brother.

Since living an intellectual life is hard work, it's encouraging to keep before one's mind and in one's heart those who have succeeded in pursuing their intellectual projects in the light of faith. St. Augustine is an obviously inspiring example, so self-reflective is he both about the faith and about living a moral life that shapes the life of a Catholic intellectual.

St. Augustine pursued his vocation to the intellectual life as a bishop of the Church, someone who is incorporated into the Church's teaching and pastoral office, whose intellectual and personal vocation included giving spiritual advice and intellectual guidance to other believers. His horizon integrated his personal life with the Lord of scripture and of history, the needs of his religious community and of the people of his city at the time of the Vandal invasion of northern Africa. To ignore any of these elements in his own formation is to leave unacknowledged the challenges that created Augustine as much as we can understand him ourselves.

The chapters that follow introduce one by one the horizons of meaning and living given us by apostolicity in the Church, now inserted into aggressively secularized contexts, even in the Church. In particular, the evolution of the university and other culture forming institutions has brought the faithful intellectual into worlds often unanticipated fifty years ago. Finally, as already recognized, the Church's own life cannot be understood without consideration of how both the Second Vatican Council and the exercise of the papal office have changed our common intellectual and spiritual life.

In tracing in my own mind my personal integration of intellectual growth and the spiritual life, the notion of horizon in a nontechnical sense showed me some of the turns and twists in my experience and was large enough to accommodate the inward attention needed to show how I've tried to integrate the various elements of my life with God and neighbor. Whom we pray for and the events included in our prayer tell us how broad and deep is the horizon of our life at any one time. Too often, growth is reduced to collecting experiences: "I did this and then studied that," as if life were a bag to be filled with particulars of our programming rather than a gift that we are given in the hope that, with the help of God's grace, we will rise to each new idea, event, and person as the years go by. Pope Francis often contrasts our planning with God's providence.

God is a God of surprises, Pope Francis explains, and the final horizon is God's infinite love. It can never be completely responded to; but as the years here grow shorter, it fills in with the realization that, just as we pray to see God face to face, so God wants to see us face to face. We give him our time, which is all that we have, and he takes the gift and calls us when he is ready to do so. In the end, that is all that there is, and everything is summed up and integrated in that vision and desire.

Francis Cardinal George, OMI
FEBRUARY 22, 2015
FEAST OF THE CHAIR OF ST. PETER

Acknowledgments

MANY HAVE CONTRIBUTED to my thinking through the topics of these essays, and, while their contributions have been very different, I wish to thank them all with all my heart. Influences on my mind and heart who have opened horizons for integration begin with some early teachers and extend through the years to directors of academic theses and to very diverse thinkers, whose paths of reflection I have not always followed but whose conversation I have been privileged to join. More directly, for some of the essays presented here, I have profited by contributions and corrections from the late Fr. Edward Oakes, SJ, from Fr. Robert Barron, Prof. Michael Baxter, Dr. Robert Royal, Sr. Sara Butler, MSBT, Fr. Matthew Lamb, Fr. Louis Cameli, Fr. Guy Mansini, Dr. Lawrence Welch, Prof. David Solomon, Fr. Thomas Baima, Prof. Paul Griffiths, and Prof. Pauline Viviano. Closer to home, this work would never have been completed without the help of Ms. Marie Knoll and Fr. Daniel Flens.

From the Lumen Christi Institute, based at the University of Chicago, Mr. Thomas Levergood has been a friendly critic and persistent mover, keeping me at work and providing a liaison with the Catholic University of America Press. Fr. Paul Mankowski, SJ, also at the Lumen Christi Institute, has done both the first and the penultimate editing of this book; Timothy Kirchoff has checked and standardized the references. Finally, allow me to thank those at the Catholic University of America Press who have shown interest in what I have written and whose careful work on the final text have put it in good order. I am grateful to Dr. Trevor Lipscombe, Theresa Walker, and Aldene Fredenburg for bringing the text into printable form. I realize how very many others I have not mentioned, including those who would be surprised to be listed as shapers of my outlook, since I have often disagreed with them, even as I learned from them how to live as a disciple of the Lord.

A GODLY HUMANISM

CHAPTER I

Saints in Catholic
Intellectual Life

THE FULL BODY OF REFLECTION on the truths of the Catholic faith represents the collected wisdom of intelligent and holy men and women from every part of the world over two millennia. Its tributaries include thousands of years of ancient Jewish experience as well as the cultures of Mesopotamia and Egypt; it draws on the entire heritage of classical Greece and Rome, the civilizations of the Middle Ages, the Renaissance, the Enlightenment, the scientific revolution, romanticism, modernism, and our globalized postmodern culture. Briefly put, there is nothing quite like it.

The Catholic intellectual tradition is universal in scope and synthetic in purpose. It aims to show the unity of reason in its ceaselessly self-critical stance, and it proposes to unite faith and reason in mutual complementarity. On occasions, the union has been effected too quickly or not critically enough; but always there is an attempt to synthesize. Even when the Catholic cannot foresee the imminent achievement of the synthesis, there is a belief that it can and will be done, because the God who reveals himself in history is the same God who reveals himself in nature, and, therefore, the one truth can't be in contradiction to the other.

This tradition, though founded on some simple truths of the Gospel, cannot by its nature be a simple thing. It has had to address many questions — many *kinds* of questions. For example, early Christians had to think carefully about the relationship of the Church to the Roman commonwealth, avoiding the pattern common in human history wherein the gods of the locale were closely associated — and sometimes identified — with its rulers. In spite of all subsequent developments after Christianity became the official religion of the Roman Empire, the faith has always carried within it a critical distance toward every political order. It knows that some things do not and never can belong to Caesar. Church and state therefore continue a conversation without a collapse, on either religious or political terms, of one entity into the other.

At the same time, the Church early on began to make use of Greco-Roman culture with its highly developed tools of analysis and expression. In the nineteenth century, under the impulse of hyper-Protestant and skeptical scholarship, this process was often represented as an improper Hellenizing or paganizing of Christianity, as if it were better for the Church to remain without cultural or intellectual elaboration. Professor Robert Wilken has recast that old argument. Christians, he says, naturally began appropriating the best thought they could find, and "At the same time, one observes again and again that Christian thinking, while working within patterns of thought and conceptions rooted in Greco-Roman culture, transformed them so profoundly that in the end something quite new came into being."[1]

This process is not merely of historical interest; the Church has always maintained that Christ came into the world "in the fullness of time," which is to say at the proper moment for the proclamation and spread of the Gospel, including in that fullness the political and cultural conditions of the classical world with its search for universalism in thought and in governance. Pope Benedict XVI emphasized the importance of this fact in his 2006 lecture at the University of Regensburg: his aim was to remind his old university — and all of us — of the necessary connection between faith and reason. He proposed an understanding of the role of history common to Jewish and Christian self-understanding. He said, "The encounter between the biblical message and Greek thought did not happen by chance. The vision of St. Paul, who saw the roads to Asia barred and in a

1. Robert Louis Wilken, *The Spirit of Early Christian Thought: Seeking the Face of God* (New Haven: Yale University Press, 2003), xvii.

dream saw a Macedonian man plead with him: 'Come over to Macedonia and help us!' [see *Acts* 16:6–10] — the vision can be interpreted as a 'distillation' of the intrinsic necessity of a rapprochement between biblical faith and Greek inquiry."[2] His purpose was to show that violence ensues when faith is not interpreted by reason and that violence ensues when reason creates its own secular utopias uncriticized by faith.

Pope Benedict understood that some parts of the Christian contact with the Greek heritage cannot be exported everywhere or entirely preserved. But there are other parts — the way that the great "I AM" on Mount Horeb anticipated and engaged Greek metaphysics, for instance, or the translation of the Old Testament from Hebrew into Greek — that are not merely accidental to the development of the faith. He said, "A profound encounter of faith and reason is taking place here, an encounter between genuine enlightenment and revealed religion."[3] In the Letter to the Romans, St. Paul calls Christian worship *logike latreia*, worship in harmony with the *logos*, presupposing that human reason is modeled on and judged by the Word made flesh.

Pope Benedict points to three phases of an improp-

2. Benedict XVI, "Faith, Reason, and the University: Memories and Reflections," lecture at Regensburg University, September, 12, 2006, *The Holy See*, http://w2.vatican.va/content/benedict-xvi/en/speeches/2006/september/documents/hf_ben-xvi_spe_20060912_university-regensburg.html.

3. Ibid.

er de-Hellenization of Christianity. The first took place at the Reformation, when some Protestants threw out all philosophical reflection on revelation in favor of *sola scriptura* — the axiom that Holy Scripture was the sole and sufficient rule of faith. This was understandable, perhaps, as a desire to return to Gospel sources too often obscured; but in some cases it involved a wholesale rejection of the cooperation of faith and reason. A second phase emerged in the nineteenth century with liberal rationalists like Adolf von Harnack, who set up human reason as the measure of revelation and theological thought in a desire to make these fit with what he assumed were the inescapable demands of modern philosophy and science, including Immanuel Kant's restrictions on what counted as reason at all. We have seen since then that the "radius of reason" to which such figures appealed was limited, not to say stunted. Finally, in line with the cultural pluralism of the postmodern West, some have argued that the first inculturation of Christianity into the Greco-Roman world was not part of God's design but a mere accident, one particular expression of faith arbitrarily refracted through one particular culture, which may legitimately be rejected in favor of going back to Gospel sources and restarting the whole process in whatever culture the innovators find themselves.

This notion of an abstract faith universally and identically insertable into any and every culture was proposed about thirty years ago and has since been seen to be illusory. While we must appropriate God's revelation to the Jewish people into our own self-understanding in order to read the New Testament well, we cannot simply posit the manifold cultures of Africa and Asia as functional equivalents of the Old Covenant so as to inject the Gospel into them.

Such intuitions about inculturation, Pope Benedict argued at Regensburg, are not entirely false, but they are not exactly true, either. The New Testament was written in Greek, and the decisions that believers made about the importance of reason in the early Christian centuries are a permanent part of our faith and of our intellectual tradition. In that perspective, the purported antagonism between faith and scientific reason must be seen as an aberration that fails either by excluding religion from the rational or by consigning religion to merely local cultures as a species of folklore. Paradoxically, the claims of a reduced reason to be more truly universal harm both faith and reason as global human values:

In the Western world it is widely held that only positivistic reason and the forms of philosophy based on it are universally valid. Yet the world's profoundly religious cultures see this exclusion of the divine from the universality of reason as an attack on their most profound convictions. A [form of] reason that is deaf to the divine and that relegates religion into the realm of subcultures is incapable of entering into the dialogue of cultures.[4]

The ample realm of *logos* is the place where true human dialogue has to take place, Pope Benedict told his listeners at Regensburg University: "To rediscover it constantly is the great task of the university."[5]

The life of the mind, or the effort to know and live according to the divine *logos*, does not take place only within universities. The two most important figures in Western history — Jesus and Socrates — were not university professors. They each talked about truth but took no payment for what they taught. They inspired disciples who carried on their missions down to the present day, though both were tried, convicted, and put to death in their own cultures. In direct and indirect ways, they each began a conversation that has not ended — because it cannot end. Socrates modeled the rational inquiry into the nature of things that humbly opened itself toward religious truths. In the *Phaedo*, for example, Plato portrays Socrates as discussing life after death and the immortality of the soul with his friends just before he is executed. When they are not convinced or consoled he tells them that it is the part of the philosopher "to take whatever human doctrine is best and

4. Ibid.
5. Ibid.

hardest to disprove and, embarking upon it as upon a raft, sail upon it through life in the midst of dangers, unless he can sail upon some stronger vessel, some divine reason (*logos*) and make his voyage more safely and securely."[6] In older translations, *logos* was often translated as "revelation" in this passage, a bit of an anachronism but one that fit the case. After all, it was the revelation of the Oracle of Delphi, that he was "the wisest of men," that got Socrates thinking about how he really knew nothing. That humble acknowledgment was the only way in which he would call himself wise.

It is not hard to see how the part of Greek culture that was influenced by Socrates and Plato had natural affinities with Christian revelation. Once our Lord had appeared in this world, nothing could ever be the same: "he spoke as one possessing authority," even in the view of some of the Jews who were authorities in the Sanhedrin. They were not able to defend him from others who resisted the irruption of the divine into what they thought was an already complete religious system or from Roman colonial authorities who wanted to maintain civil peace at all costs. But no other figure in the history of the world has pronounced such striking statements — "Before Abraham was, I AM"; "I am the way,

6. Plato, *Phaedo* 85 c–d., trans. Robert Royal; see Royal, *The God That Did Not Fail: How Religion Built and Sustains the West* (New York: Encounter, 2006), 4.

the truth, and the life"; "He who has seen me has seen the Father"; and perhaps most shocking of all, "Your sins are forgiven." All this, too, transpired outside institutions of higher learning.

And yet all this has immense importance for those institutions, the universities, that were created in the Middle Ages by the Church and after that, for the most part, sponsored by Catholic or Protestant initiatives. State colleges, which some see as the norm, are a relatively recent creation. These too serve a purpose, but often one different from the original notion of a university — a place where everything is open to intellectual scrutiny. The Catholic intellectual tradition provides us with an already developed body of thought tested by many different people in a wide variety of circumstances over many centuries. While we have to learn about life and love and intellectual achievement for ourselves, we do not have to learn the most important truths without reliable teachers from the tradition.

In such teaching and learning, both professors and students are part of a common enterprise — a tradition that shapes a community. What we find in the indisputable genius of major carriers of the Catholic intellectual tradition, Augustine and Aquinas, we may discover in numerous other figures across the ages: in Justin Martyr, Origen, Ambrose, Jerome, Benedict, Francis of Assisi, Dominic Guzman, Catherine of Siena, Nicholas of

Cusa, Erasmus, Thomas More, Ignatius of Loyola, Robert Bellarmine, Teresa of Avila, Therese of Lisieux, John of the Cross, Francis de Sales, Pascal, Chateaubriand, John Henry Newman, Jacques Maritain, Edith Stein, Hans Urs von Balthasar, Karol Wojtyła, and Joseph Ratzinger. All of them are marked by the Catholic embrace of both faith and reason and are quite deft in drawing on great secular thinkers like Socrates, Plato, Aristotle, the Stoics, Cicero, and Plotinus in the ancient world and Descartes, Kant, Hegel, Bergson, Husserl, Heidegger, Wittgenstein, and many others in the modern world. The Catholic intellectual tradition is almost by definition an education in great books — and great souls.

Let us look for a moment at the tradition in universities and in the various disciplines. So rich is this tradition that at times it runs the risk of getting lost or losing its cogency in the sheer welter of different schools and truths that it harbors within itself. Too often what is valued in academic life is almost entirely criticism and creativity, not homage and fidelity to what has been discovered and found sound.

A very good example in recent formulation of this academic stance appeared in 2007 in the "Final Report of the Task Force on General Education," written by a curricular committee at Harvard University. That committee was given the responsibility to examine the undergraduate curriculum at Harvard, but it retained enough of the old understanding of liberal education as a preparation for the life of a free human being that it distinguished such studies from professional training. Then it went on to proclaim, "The aim of a liberal education is to unsettle presumptions, to defamiliarize the familiar, to reveal what is going on beneath and behind appearances, to disorient young people."[7] True enough up to a point; it was the exact thing that Socrates used to do with the youth of Athens. But Socrates would never have called the "*aim* of liberal education" to be unsettling, defamiliarizing, and disorienting the youth of Athens. He wanted to know the truth, and he did not assume that the truth would turn out to be the kind of politicized goal evident in the Harvard Task Force's belief that a liberal education will "reveal what's going on beneath and behind appearances."

Catholic intellectual tradition is quite a bit more radical and unsettling than that, even if it appears quite settled and familiar at the outset. It believes that God himself has communicated to us truths about matter that are beyond our natural capacities to understand but that are essential to living a good life here and to attaining eternal life in the world to come. Those who think that our tradition accepted this revelation as settled and familiar thereby show themselves to be quite

7. "Report of the Task Force on General Education" (Cambridge, Mass.: President and Fellows of Harvard College, 2007), 1–2.

provincial and unfamiliar with the truly immense critical and scholarly labors applied to the faith by legions of very careful reasoners. When St. Paul proclaimed Christ on the Areopagus in ancient Athens, the jaded Athenian intellectuals had the same reaction as many of their descendants today. But from that revealed seed, as we have seen, several subsequent civilizations arose. The Harvard approach results in a worldly wise skepticism about our immediate American culture. St. Augustine's Platonism or Aquinas's Platonic-Augustinian-Aristotelianism poses a critique not only of our mainstream culture but of the critical categories of Harvard curricular committees. The reason for this is simple: the main figures in the Catholic intellectual tradition want to know the truth, and they believe that knowing the truth is the purpose of education at all times and in all places. Furthermore, they believe that truth exists, however difficult it may be to achieve a grasp of it.

The Catholic intellectual tradition makes its greatest contributions when it remains itself, when it offers as much as possible of the rich and varied heritage with which it has been blessed. Tradition, as the philologists remind us, means a "handing on" of what we have received. As we can see from the tradition, that handing on is not the mere mechanical reproduction of thoughts from one generation to the next. Handing on means, inevitably, the active engagement of currents of thought, first by teachers and then by learners, since the tradition has developed. But both the contemplation and the passing on, to say nothing of the appropriation, are all carried on by living human beings who try to discern the particular way in which the tradition may come to be incarnated in new situations in different cultures. In that sense, our tradition values newness and creativity but not the radical break that modern creativity assumes; rather, it requires the kind of creativity that recognizes its connection to the whole of human history, past and future, and to God himself. A tradition like ours that has looked deeply at the most basic questions — *Who am I? Where have I come from and where am I destined to go? Why is there evil? What is there after this life?*, as John Paul II listed them at the beginning of his great encyclical *Fides et ratio* (1998) — is not mired in some settled and familiar backwater but is engaged with intellectual work that has not gone out of date because it cannot as long as human beings inhabit this earth.

The Catholic Intellectual Tradition in the Church

The Catholic intellectual tradition has, as part of its proper vocation, an importance for both the Church and society. The Catholic intellectual tradition derives from the Church's self-understanding. If the Catholic Church did not value both faith *and* reason and were content to remain behind cloistered walls without engaging the world, she would not even have an intellectual tradition or feel a need to develop intellectual tools capable of meeting contemporary intellectual challenges. But we are members of a *communio* of persons throughout time and extending into eternity that has always taken our Lord's words at the end of the Gospel according to St. Matthew to mean that its universal mission covers the farthest ends of the earth and every dimension of human life. The intellectual tradition of our Catholic faith therefore serves the Church in three principal ways.

First, it is constantly engaged in making clear that the tenets of the faith are not opposed to reason. This may seem an ill-conceived or fruitless task, but it is really a fundamental contribution to the Church's mission. Revealed truths like the Holy Trinity or the Incarnation or the real Eucharistic Presence are, properly speaking, mysteries of faith. They do not present us with intellectual puzzles that can be solved but with truths of the faith that are to be contemplated. Nevertheless, reason has a role in helping to define what each of these mysteries and tenets of the faith is and what it is not. Rationalists fail to understand the proper bounds of reason, however, when they believe it must prove a mystery of faith. This is not some modern realization that philosophy has come to in the wake of a figure like Kant. In the first book of the *Summa contra gentiles*, St. Thomas Aquinas warns against using the arguments he advances there to *prove* the truth of the faith to non-Christians. If we do that, he says, they will think that the faith rests on the weak arguments that we human beings can bring to Christian apologetics. Aquinas recommends instead that we pursue various rational paths to keep the mind open to the action of the Holy Spirit, who is the real agent of conversion in any of us. Newman said that you convert no one with a syllogism, but you have to make them nonetheless.

Second, this delimitation provides a useful caution for believers already within the Church. Particularly in our time, when many are troubled about their faith because they are constantly told that faith is "irrational," a careful delineation of what pure reason or empirical science really tells us is of no small service. The answers that Christian reason has given to these questions in St. Paul and Augustine, in Dante and Thomas à Kempis, in Aquinas and Hans Urs von Balthasar are quite illuminating, where they are known. Often people don't bother to know them because the philosophical methodology that the modern sciences use presupposes that only matter is active, that spirit does not have power and, therefore, if one attributes power or action to a spirit, he is immediately beyond rationality and into superstition.

The historical figures that I've just mentioned help

us to understand the relationship of love and freedom, something often missing in modern culture. The new, more militant atheists such as Richard Dawkins, Daniel Dennett, and Sam Harris sometimes suggest that there is no such thing as human freedom because everything is determined by the iron laws of physics and biology. If so, it is difficult to understand why they often make angry arguments against the faith since, after all, believers would then be just as much a product of impersonal forces as are unbelievers. Our tradition opens up the spaces where freedom, courage, sympathy, and love — for which the narrow world of the atheist has little or no room — can exist and flourish together. The Church needs members who can articulate these truths in a way that shows the right and wrong applications of reason to human concerns.

Third, the Catholic intellectual tradition helps the Church understand what she has to say affirmatively about human concerns and their divine foundations. It is one sign of the fertility of Christian belief and thought that we have absorbed not only the thought of Plato and Aristotle, the two great philosophers of antiquity, but the various currents of modern thought, insofar as they can be reconciled with revelation. To the surprise of some Catholics themselves, there is actually quite a bit of convergence between any authentic philosophy that tries to explain human existence and the faith tradition that unites us to the apostles. When existentialism became a powerful current in France, for example, Catholic thinkers uncovered the existentialist elements already present in Augustine, Pascal, and even Aquinas. After two thousand years, there is little that our tradition has not in some sense already seen and that it cannot put to good use for Christ's mystical body, the Church.

Like the Ethiopian eunuch who could not understand the prophetic word unless someone explained it to him,[8] we have much need of convinced and skillful laborers in the vineyard who can bring the Catholic intellectual tradition into a variety of contexts where dialogue is languishing now for want of real understanding. It is not easy to master even one segment of that tradition — and it is even harder to make the imaginative effort to see how it enters into the unique circumstances in which God has placed us in our time. But those circumstances are not entirely unprecedented. We have been blessed with ancestors and, even today, produce contemporaries who point the way toward faithfulness to the past, engagement in the present, and confidence about the future. They carry the tradition.

8. See Acts 8:31–35.

CHAPTER 2

An Integrated Life

THE CATHOLIC INTELLECTUAL TRADITION begins
with Catholics who become intellectuals or intellectuals
who become disciples of Christ in his body the Church.
But because both discipleship and the intellectual life
are universal in scope, the life and worth of Catholic intellectuals is lived in the Church and in society at
large. The institutionalization of that conversation between the human intellect and the faith that comes to
us from the apostles began with the conversion of philosophers in ancient Rome and moved, over the centuries, from their schools and their coteries of disciples to
the monastic schools during feudal times, then, with
the refounding of cities, to the cathedral schools and
to the universities, and now to the communications
industry with newspapers and then radio, television,
and the Internet. In all these places and through many
conversations, Catholic intellectuals have grappled
with translating the doctrine of the faith from the languages of revelation, Hebrew, Aramaic, and Greek, to

various vernaculars. They have had to ask about rules of evidence and types of certitude and the differences between sciences of faith and those of nature and have had to come to terms with the moral codes that flowed from the vision of faith in contrast with the ways of life that were being called to conversion.

To illustrate this conversation, rooted in personal life and carrying universal significance, we can hardly do better than examine the contribution of St. Augustine to the Catholic faith and to the relation between his theology of Church and its relation to the ecumenical movement of our day. This is the search for the visible unity of all those who call Jesus Lord. Because continuity shines through difference, St. Augustine, more than almost anyone else, has shaped the Catholic intellectual tradition; his influence on the Church and on Western civilization can scarcely be exaggerated. He lived and wrote toward the end of the Western Roman Empire as it was being driven back into itself because of invasions from the outside. Augustine tried to put together what he knew from faith, what he knew from reason, and what he was experiencing from history and from his own inner conversion. These were sources, therefore, of the inner conversation that expressed itself in his voluminous writings.

What was God telling Augustine from the depths of his own conscience? What was God telling the world by allowing the Roman Empire (the *oekumene*) to collapse? What could one say in Augustine's time about the divine self-revelation four or five centuries earlier in the historical events surrounding the passion, death, and resurrection of Jesus and the written witness to this in the inspired books of the New Testament? How were all these elements to be put together into a tradition that would establish a perduring connection between faith and reason?

Augustine insisted that the authority of faith and the questionings of reason are parallel routes to the same truth. Reason for St. Augustine was best represented by the philosopher Plato and the neo-Platonists after him. Augustine put a well-established intellectual tradition, the Platonic tradition, into conversation with the Catholic faith; he saw them as talking back and forth, the one enlightening the other, without necessarily coming to a complete synthesis. Faith and reason have a dialectical relationship in Augustine — that is, a relationship of critical engagement and mutual influence — but believers have the sure conviction that one truth cannot contradict another, for the source of any truth is always God. In coming to a resolution expressive of the truth of faith and the arguments of reason, Augustine had to face both adversaries of the faith and opponents of his understanding of human reason. It is necessary to study his adversaries, because one thinks more clearly when arguing with opponents. The great service of adversaries is that they force one to ask, "Why do I think that? What's the evidence for that? Are there some canons of evidence that enable me to defend what I've said against those who would contest it?"

St. Augustine was an influential bishop and a great intellectual. He engaged the schools of thought, the intellectual traditions of his own time, and the expressions of faith that were not Catholic. Augustine argued with Stoics who taught that nature can be known rather exactly and with a great deal of ease. He also faced skeptics who believed just the opposite — that one couldn't know anything with confidence, that what one grasped were a few fleeting truths that were here today and gone tomorrow. Augustine, in the face of these opinions, argued that human beings might use some authority, such as the teachings of Jesus Christ, to point the way to truth. But then the mind continues with its own questions, formulating its own queries, following its own desire to know. Such parallelism wasn't a contradiction. Even when one couldn't put everything together in synthesis, one continued on the several paths of inquiry.

One can use authority to point the way to truth because the truths that are given to us, even by natural reasoning and by logic, are always arrived at with great difficulty. And if God in his graciousness reveals certain absolute truths to us, we have a head start on the path to truth. Faith gives us the ability to penetrate even natural truths, using natural reason more thoroughly and effectively, avoiding many errors. To preach the Christian Gospel, Augustine linked arms with Platonic ethics and metaphysics. He used philosophy's negative impersonal language that leaves God as the great unknown but names him nonetheless and therefore makes a truth claim. Augustine brought that Platonic meaning together with the Biblical concept — itself more positive — of God as love, as power, as justice, as forgiveness in their transcendent source.

It is cardinal to Christian theism that the mystery of God is known not only as we can reason about it and come to it ourselves but also by God's self-disclosure, in which a personal God does not unveil a cosmological principle, but makes known to others what they could not find out about him by themselves.

Augustine was a man who searched his own inner spirit with a persistence and penetration that intellectuals were not to see again before the age of modernity. His own consciousness and his own conscience provide insights into the nature of God. He admitted that one can learn something about God through physical nature. To gaze at the sky on a starry night can move us to gratitude for something that we know we didn't create. That's one of the lines of rational argument for the existence of God. But Augustine held that even if you can argue in that fashion — and many of the Stoics did so — that doesn't tell you who God is from within God's own self. Of course, one can learn about God as it were "by reputation" — from what other persons tell us about his nature — but Augustine pointed out that that way also presents a lot of wrong ideas about God. Therefore, in his graciousness, God has revealed an interior or subjective side of himself, preeminently and definitively in Jesus of Nazareth.

The eternal Word — the great beginning of the conversation that is the mystery of the Godhead from all eternity in the Holy Trinity — is made flesh and is therefore available to us for our conversation in human words. The interior life of God isn't available to reason; it must come to us only from divine self-revelation. In order to have a more complete understanding of God, Augustine attempted a partial synthesis of philosophy — that is, science or natural reason — with theology, the science of faith based on a personal assent to God's self-revelation.

Augustine embraced all the conversations that shaped the culture and the shared life of his own day. His attempt at synthesis, limited by his dialectical methodology, remained for centuries the most exhaustive form of philosophical speculation known in the West. It was a direct answer to the challenge of one of the early Church fathers, Tertullian, who wanted to distinguish faith and reason to the point of separation. He famously asked, "What does Athens have to do with Jerusalem?" What does the academy and intellectual work have to do with the Church and the faith? That challenge of fideism — we might call it fundamentalism today — is much alive in some religious traditions, but it is foreign to Catholicism. Augustine also had to argue with the Gnostics, and they too are back in fashion today. Gnostics taught that we're saved not because of a person, Jesus of Nazareth, and our relationship to him, but because we have esoteric *gnosis* — knowledge. This enlightenment doesn't come from personal reason; rather, it's a secret knowledge that is handed on among the Gnostics from generation to generation. Such knowledge isn't able to be criticized by reason, nor does one use the intellect to understand it more deeply. Only if one is part of the group — the *cognoscenti*, the Gnostics — can one truly understand what reality is all about. Augustine, because he believed that knowledge from reason was true knowledge and also believed that revelation tells us that we're saved not by an idea but by a person, Jesus Christ, condemned the Gnostics for sinning against both God and human reason.

Augustine had to face the Gnostic challenge, and he insisted that Christian faith can defend the reliability of natural reason while surpassing its limits. The innate genius of Christianity and the insight of the fathers of the Church recognized that faith vindicates philosophy — and human reason itself — against the claims of esoteric *gnosis* to be "beyond" the flaws of factual falsehood or self-contradiction. Faith protects and defends critical philosophy because faith needs critical intelligence. Faith needs philosophers, people who question and who seek, so that the ongoing development of an ever-deeper understanding of the mysteries of the faith can continue. That is why the vocation of theologians is honored in the Church. It is not questioning, Augustine said, that creates obstacles for the faith; rather, it is intellectual closure that holds that truth is unreachable by reason or isn't worth striving for at all that enfeebles belief. Faith doesn't destroy either science or philosophy; rather, it champions both in the name of faith itself.

Interestingly, how St. Augustine's teaching on the Church and the communion of saints informs our understanding of the ecumenical venture speaks directly to his pastoral synthesis of faith and reason. In the first seven or eight centuries of the Church's history, most theologians — Augustine included — were bishops, pastors responsible for the unity of the Church. In the Middle Ages, most theologians were priests, usually monks or friars in a religious order like the Benedictines, Dominicans, or Franciscans. In modern times, most theologians, including Catholics, are professors in universities. In a university context, the conversation continues among believers, whether bishops, priests, or lay people, but the speakers have a different set of responsibilities. Bishops, as noted above, are responsible for the unity of the Church. Priests are responsible for the people who come to them, particularly in Eucharistic communities called parishes. Professors are responsible first of all to their discipline and to their peers within their academic discipline. The concerns and the tonality that are brought to that conversation between faith and reason change as each participant changes the context. The canons of evidence are differently configured, and the burden of proof is differently assigned. In some cases the university has replaced the faith community, the Church, as the guardian of theological methodology, if not of truth.

Augustine was aware of the multiple contexts in which people carried on the conversation between faith and reason. He lived in the period of transition between the world of classical Greco-Roman culture, with its weighty intellectual tradition, and the world of the Middle Ages, when, with the collapse of the Roman Empire, many of the classics of antiquity were destroyed or lost. Those that survived were saved in the monasteries and in virtue of the scholarship that the monasteries sustained. Augustine was both a bishop and a monk. He formed a monastic community around his cathedral residence in Hippo in northern Africa and wrote a rule for his monks that came to be adopted as the rule of life for many orders and religious communities over the centuries since his death. His way of life protects the faith and fosters its dialogue with reason.

Centuries after St. Augustine's death, the figure of Martin Luther stands as the hinge between the medieval and the modern world, as Augustine was the hinge between the classical epoch and the medieval. Luther was both a monk (in fact, an Augustinian monk) and a professor. He left the monastic life when he left the Catholic Church. But even before his excommunication by Pope Leo X in 1521, Luther was a professor of the Old Testament at Wittenburg University, and he held that position until his death. In his own mind, and for those who followed him, Luther reconfigured the relation between faith and reason.

On one level these developments are mere social arrangements. They take on a larger significance when we notice the unraveling within Christianity of its institutional order and of the belief structures that sustained them and that they protected. This is the concern of ecumenism: how do you knit together into a functioning whole a Christian movement that has unraveled? What caused it to unravel in the first place? Jaroslav Pelikan, in the preface to the fifth volume of his book *The Christian Tradition: A History of the Development of the Doctrine*, observes, "the modern period in the history of Christian doctrine may be defined as the time when

AN INTEGRATED LIFE 27

doctrines that had been assumed more than debated for most of Christian history were themselves called into question: the idea of revelation, the uniqueness of Christ, the authority of Scripture, the expectation of life after death, even the very transcendence of God."[1] Speaking still of the beginning of the modern age, Pelikan added:

It was also a time when the relation between the three terms "believe, teach and confess," with which the first volume of this work opened in defining Christian doctrine was basically revised: theologians often "confessed" more than they "believed," perhaps more than they "taught."[2]

St. Augustine would have been utterly baffled by this division between personal belief, professional teaching, and the public expression or confessing of faith. So should be all Catholics. At the ordination of a deacon the bishop gives him this charge:

Receive the Gospel of Christ, whose herald you now are. Believe what you read, teach what you believe, and practice what you teach.

Here we approach the central reason that the ecumenical movement has come to a pause, if not something of a standstill: ecumenism *should* be about those secondary doctrines that divide Christians, such as the

1. Jaroslav Pelikan, *The Christian Tradition: A History of the Development of Doctrine* (Chicago: University of Chicago Press, 1991), 5:viii.
2. Ibid., 5:viii–ix.

nature of justification and the authority of the Bishop of Rome. But the lull in ecumenical energy comes from unwillingness or inability to confront the dilemma posed by Pelikan. Once the primary doctrines, like the uniqueness of Christ, the transcendence of God, and life after death, begin to be called into question, the doctrinal dialogues are no longer geared up to achieve what the challenges to ecumenism make necessary.

The thinking and the witness of St. Augustine are apposite here. One of the reasons that the transcendence of God — as an example of a primary doctrine — has been called into question is because a transcendent God is felt to be too "imperial," too distant, too outside of ourselves. To that complaint Augustine has a brilliant answer, the one he gave to the pagans of his day in one of his most famous books, *The City of God*:

It is nothing but folly, nothing but pitiable aberration, to humble yourself before a being you would hate to resemble in the conduct of your life and to worship one whom you would refuse to imitate. For surely the supremely important thing in religion is to model oneself on the object of one's worship.[3]

For Augustine nothing is more important than worship; indeed, nothing is more *fulfilling* than worship. This centrality is acknowledged in the goal of the modern ecumenical movement: the eventual common wor-

3. Augustine, *The City of God* VIII.17, trans. Henry Bettensen (Harmondsworth: Penguin, 1972), 324.

ship and inter-communion among all who recognize Jesus as Lord must be the final goal.

Augustine said famously in his *Confessions*, "You have made us and drawn us to Yourself, and our heart is unquiet until it rests in you."[4] True religion can start only when we recognize that we are not God but are nonetheless closer to him than we are to ourselves and, if divided from God, then we are also divided from ourselves. That's a datum of self-consciousness. It doesn't come from reflecting on the cosmological arguments for the existence of God. It's a particularly Augustinian argument.

But who exactly is the God who created us for himself? None other than the triune God revealed in Christ Jesus. And that brings us to the next central doctrinal issue, the uniqueness of Christ. St. Paul says in his letter to the Colossians, "For all things were created by [Christ] and for him" (Col 1:16). Just as our hearts are restless until they rest in God, so too do they remain restless until they rest in Christ. This is because we do not just need a knowledge of God — a *gnosis*; much more, we need *redemption*, a new relation effected only through Jesus Christ. As Augustine says in *Sermon 90*:

4. Augustine, *Confessions* I.I.I., in *The Works of St. Augustine: A Translation for the 21st Century*, part 1, *Books*, vol. 1, *The Confessions*, trans. Maria Boulding, OSB (Hyde Park, N.Y.: New City Press, 1997), 39.

Consider our species, our human race.... One man begot us to sin and to death, and yet [he did so] as one race, yet as all neighbors to each other, yet as not only like each other but as all related to each other. One man [Christ] came against one man [Adam]; against one man who *scattered* came one who *gathered*. In the same way against one man who killed came one man who made alive. For "just as in Adam all die, so in Christ shall all be made alive" (1 Cor 15:22). But just as everyone who is born of that man dies, so too everyone who believes in Christ is made alive.[5]

The relevance of Augustine's teaching and witness for contemporary ecumenism is evident in the painfully obvious consequences of weakening the doctrine of the uniqueness of Christ. Insofar as ecumenism is infected with a Christological pluralism that says one Christian group's or one particular Christian's sense of Christ is as valid as another's — since each "savior figure" is a "savior figure" for that particular religion — then ecumenism loses any point of reference that can serve to unify both belief (a way of thinking) and communities based on belief in Christ (ways of living).

When the Catholic Church reiterated the teaching of St. Paul and of St. Augustine about who Christ is in the document *Dominus Jesus* (2000),[6] a firestorm of contro-

5. Augustine, *Sermon 90.7*, in *Works of St. Augustine*, part 3, *Sermons*, vol. 3, *Sermons 51–94*, trans. Edmund Hill, OP (Brooklyn, N.Y.: New City Press, 1991), 452; emphases added.

6. Congregation for the Doctrine of the Faith, *Dominus Jesus* (Rome: Typis Polyglottis Vaticanis, 2000).

versy broke out, with critics claiming that the Church was abandoning both interreligious dialogue and ecumenism at the same time. The problem of defining the Church's beliefs is not just doctrinal, although it is fundamentally that; it is also historical. Augustine knew that history ultimately means what God remembers; but for us history is marked not only by remembering but by forgetting. Catholics remember some historical events, other Christians remember other things, and some of it almost everyone forgets. The dialogue has to be not only about doctrine but also about history.

Far from representing a denial of the elements of goodness in other religions and, still less, far from denying the elements of Christian truth among non-Catholic Christians, this truth of the uniqueness of Jesus Christ is the pledge of the Church's *openness* to the world and the basis for her charter of dialogue with fellow Christians and all persons of good will. This is the teaching of the Second Vatican Council and was the whole point of Augustine's *Sermon 90* just quoted. Note how Augustine says that in Adam we are all one race to begin with, all neighbors to each other, not only like each other but, in fact, related to each other. Augustine makes the point even more explicitly in his *Commentary on Psalm 95 (96)*:

"For with righteousness shall he judge the world." Not a part of it only, for it was not merely a part that he redeemed; the whole of the world is his to judge, since for the whole did he pay the price [of his Blood]. You have heard what the Gospel has to say, that when he comes "He shall gather together the elect from the four winds" (Mk 13:27). He gathers all the elect from the four winds, that is to say from the whole world. Now Adam's name, as I have said more than once, means in Greek the whole world. For there are four letters in his name: A, D, A, and M; and with the Greeks the four quarters of the world have these initial Letters.... Adam is thus scattered throughout the globe. Set in one place, he fell and, as it were, broken small, he has filled the whole world. But the Divine Mercy gathered up the fragments from every side, forged them in the fire of love and welded into one what had been broken. That was a work which this Artist knew how to do! Let no one therefore give way to despair! An immense task it was indeed! But think who the artist was! He who remade [us] was himself the Maker. He who refashioned [us] was himself the Fashioner. "He shall judge the world in righteousness and the nations in this truth."[7]

How does the Church fit into all this, and what does it say to us that the "fragments" that the Lord must now gather up include a fragmented Church, torn asunder by the sins of her own children? St. Augustine says that, in the Church, the lowly human race is refashioned and recreated.[8] The French Jesuit theologian Henri de Lubac,

7. Cited in Henri de Lubac, *Catholicism: Christ and the Common Destiny of Mankind*, foreword by Joseph Cardinal Ratzinger, trans. Lancelot C. Sheppard and Sister Elizabeth England, OCD (San Francisco: Ignatius Press, 1988), 376.

8. "The very apex of authority and the whole light of reason are established in that one saving Name and in his one Church for the recreating and refashioning of the human race"; Augustine, *Letter 118*, quoted in de Lubac, *Catholicism*, 223.

in *Catholicism: Christ and the Common Destiny of Man,* comments on the line of Augustine just mentioned and the claim that the human race could be redeemed in and through the Church alone:

Surely we can find the required explanation, at least in embryo, in the traditional principle that.... the human race is one. By our fundamental nature and still more in virtue of our common destiny, we are members of the same body. Now the life of the members comes from the life of the body. How, then, can there be salvation for the members if.... the body itself were not saved? But salvation for this body, for humanity consists in receiving the form of Christ, and that is possible only through the Catholic Church. For is she not then the only complete, authoritative interpreter of Christian revelation? Is it not through her that the practice of the evangelical virtues is spread throughout the world? And, lastly, is she not responsible for realizing the spiritual unity of men insofar as they will lend themselves to it? Thus this Church, which as the invisible Body of Christ is identified with final salvation, as a visible and historical institution is the providential means of this salvation.[9]

Far from being in her true essence a stumbling block to unity, the Church must lead to that very unity. Augustine says in *Sermon 399*:

Nothing is so near, so much a neighbor, as one human being to another. But if we assume that only those born of the same parents are neighbors, let us turn our attention to Adam and Eve, and we are all brothers and sisters; brothers and sisters in-

9. De Lubac, *Catholicism*, 222–23.

deed, insofar as we are human — how much more so in that we are Christians? As regards your being human — your one father was Adam, your one mother Eve. As regards your being Christian, your one father is God, your one mother the Church.[10]

One might easily object that every human being is a member of the human race but not everyone takes the Church for his mother, so why not encourage love of neighbor without bringing God our Father into it, let alone the Church as our mother? That is where ecumenism, for many people, seems to have reached its limit. On a pragmatic level achievement of such a limited goal may sometimes be judged satisfactory; its achievement today is certainly better than living with the artificially exacerbated enmity that was common fifty or sixty years ago. But the question of what is true, what is revealed by God, is unavoidable, even in our pluralistic culture. We must try to respond in order to be faithful to the Gospel, the Gospel that Augustine believed and tirelessly preached and practiced.

St. Augustine always distinguished between the heavenly Church as the New Jerusalem and the visible Church on earth — not, to be sure, to downgrade the visible Church, but because he was aware of how much the visible Church was, as he called it, a *corpus mixtum* —

10. Augustine, *Sermon 399.3*, in *Works of St. Augustine* , part 3, *Sermons*, vol.10, *Sermons 341–400*, trans. Edmund Hill, OP (Brooklyn, N.Y.: New City Press, 1990), 460.

the body in which we convene to intermingle, in which all will be sorted out at the end of time.[11] This recognition of the ongoing sinfulness of the members of the Church was important for Augustine, especially when he did battle with the Donatists, the schismatic group that insisted that only the holy and the pure belonged to the Church. Such a view inevitably leads to sectarianism, and from there it is a short step to the kind of self-righteousness that assumes one can become quite free of sin by one's own efforts.[12] Such was the view of the Pelagians, who were Augustine's chief antagonists in the latter years of his life.

11. "This line of thought necessitates the embracing of a further paradox: if the visible Church is thus a mixed body of saints and sinners, that cannot be understood to be the case with the mystical body of those God alone knows to be His own. So we have both a 'true Church' which is 'impure' and a 'true Church' which is 'pure' and holy, existing one within the other in some ultimately perhaps indefinable relation"; Gillian R. Evans, "Augustine and the Church," in *Saint Augustine the Bishop: A Book of Essays*, ed. Fannie LeMoine and Christopher Kleinhenz (New York: Garland, 1994), 169.

12. "The Christian congregation of Hippo, then, represented the focal point of Augustine's conception of the Church of Christ, but it did not distract his gaze from the whole Catholic Church, spread from East to West. On the contrary, no Christian thinker has been more aware of the universality, of the catholicity, of the Church, than Augustine. In a sense his notion of catholicity was forced upon him by his dispute with the Donatists, who gloried in the notion that true faith had perished throughout the rest of the Christian world and remained only among themselves in Africa. Even without their challenge, Augustine would have been unable to rest content with a self-satisfied parochialism like theirs....Unlike pagan philosophy, which was the concern only of an elite, Christianity appealed to all, without any distinction of learning and ignorance"; Gerald Bonner, "Augustine's Understanding of the Church as a Eucharistic Community," in LeMoine and Kleinhenz, *Saint Augustine the Bishop*, 41–42.

To the present point, Augustine in no way wished to deny his opponents any claim at all to the truth. In fact, in a remarkable anticipation of Vatican II's teaching that Catholics should rejoice whenever they find the Gospel truths in other Christian bodies or indeed even in other religions, Augustine fully admitted that Donatists are in fact partly Catholic, just as Catholics can be partly schismatic. The noted Augustine scholar Gillian Evans said of Augustine's attitude toward the Donatists:

He was able to envisage a communion in parts, an interpenetration of the true Church with that which is not the Church truly or fully. In his book on baptism he argued against the Donatists, that the Donatists are in communion with the Catholic Church at all points where they are in agreement with it; they are in schism at the points where they disagree. Individual Christians may be partly in schism (that is, in those points at which they differ from the Catholic consensus), and partly in unity with the Catholic Church. That means that the Donatists are not wholly out of communion with the Catholics, and for this reason too their baptism need not therefore be regarded as invalid.[13]

13. Evans, "Augustine and the Church," 169. Also apposite: "Those, therefore, who have received baptism outside the fold possess nevertheless some indestructible sign of belonging to Christ. It is a badge indicating that its possessor belongs to the Church of Christ even if he received it outside the Church or has strayed from the true Church in which he received it....When members bearing the inward sign of Christ return to the Church to which they rightfully belong, they are not marked anew by baptism (*whether they received the sacrament in or outside the Catholic Church*) but are reinstated as members of the true Church of Christ and begin to exercise their duties in virtue of the deputation — the character *that they already possess*"; Stanislaus J. Grabowski, *The Church: An Introduction to the Theology of St. Augustine* (St. Louis: Herder, 1957), 418; emphases added.

In other words, when faced with sectarians the Catholic Church acts like a sect herself by denying the achievement of truths outside of her formally recognized membership. Vatican II made clear again that dissent and disobedience should not be attitudes characteristic of genuine Catholics. The Catholic Church is either universal, or she's not Catholic. The challenge is to explain that universality and show how those who are not explicitly Catholic are nonetheless in some fashion related to the Church.

Augustine did that by distinguishing in order to unite, by distinguishing the visible Church from the invisible communion of saints. "Catholics must joyfully acknowledge and esteem the truly Christian endowments from our common heritage which are to be found among our separated brethren. It is right and salutary to recognize the riches of Christ and the virtuous works in the lives of others who are bearing witness to Christ, sometimes even to the shedding of their blood. For God is always wonderful in His works and worthy of admiration."[14] Moreover, the Church extends that same gesture of confidence and serene Catholicity to members of other religions, to other faiths, when she says:

14. Vatican II, *Unitatis redintegratio*, Decree on Ecumenism §4, in *The Documents of Vatican II*, edited by Walter M. Abbott, SJ (New York: Guild Press, 1966), 349.

The Catholic Church rejects nothing which is true and holy in these religions. She looks with sincere respect upon those ways of conduct and of life, those rules and teachings which, though differing in many particulars from what she holds and sets forth, nevertheless often reflect a ray of the Truth which enlightens all men.[15]

In other words, the Church is ecumenical precisely because she is Catholic.[16] But her catholicity extends far beyond the human family currently living on this planet, for her universal membership includes the communion of saints. As Augustine himself says in Book 20 of *The City of God:*

The souls of the pious departed are not separated from the Church, which is even now the Kingdom of Christ, for otherwise no mention would be made of them at God's altar at the

15. Vatican II, *Nostra aetate*, "Declaration on the Relationship of the Church to Non-Christian Religions," cited in Abbott, *Documents of Vatican II*, 662.

16. Indeed, for Augustine, the Church, in her serene guardianship of the truth, can take even heresy in her stride: "Only because of the heretics in her midst could the Catholic Church find a more exact way to express herself in words, and the orthodox were preserved in their right-thinking because of the false thinkers among them....For example, was any complete account of the Trinity available before the Arians began to bay at it....Nor had the unity of Christ's body [the Church] been discussed in such a developed, explicit way until [the Donatists] division began to trouble the weaker brethren"; Augustine, *Expositions of the Psalms: 51–72*, at Psalm 54:22, trans. Maria Boulding, OSB (Hyde Park, N.Y.: New City Press, 2001), 74–75. Further: "For you are not to suppose, brethren, that heresies could be produced through any little souls. None save great men have been the authors of heresies"; Augustine, *Expositions of the Psalms*, at Psalm 124:5; cited in *An Augustine Synthesis*, ed. Erich Przywara, SJ (New York: Sheed and Ward, 1936), 272.

communion of the Body of Christ.... Why are such things done unless it is because the faithful are still members of this Body, even when they have departed this life?[17]

This brings us back to worship. Augustine's reference to the Eucharist is crucial, for in the Eucharist the visible Church on earth unites with the heavenly Church, the new Jerusalem on high. Both dimensions of the one Church, temporal on earth and eternal in heaven, are composed of a redeemed people, redeemed in virtue of Christ's self-sacrifice made sacramentally present in the sacrifice of the Mass. From *The City of God* again:

The whole redeemed community — that is, the congregation and fellowship of the saints — is offered to God as a universal sacrifice, through the great High Priest who offered Himself for us in His Passion "in the form of a slave" (Phil 2:7), so that we might be the Body of so great a Head. In this form He offered sacrifice, in this form He was offered up, because in this form he is the Mediator, the Priest and the Sacrifice.... This is the sacrifice of Christians, who are many, making up one body in Christ. This sacrifice the Church continually celebrates in the sacrament of the altar, well known to the faithful, in which it is shown to the Church that in the offering which she makes to God, she herself is offered.[18]

St. Augustine's mental geography continues to define the Catholic intellectual tradition and to inform

17. Augustine, *The City of God* XX.9.2, 916.
18. Ibid., X.10.6, 380.

the Church's teaching on the relationship between the Church and the world and her relationship to all those who would call Christ Lord. Augustine reflected on the nature of the Church in the midst of the collapse of the ancient order, a collapse he attributed to the worship of false gods. The Second Vatican Council similarly was called in the midst of the collapse of the colonial order after several world wars and conflicts based on racial differences, class antagonisms, nationalistic and other ideologically fueled upheavals, and divisions that prevented us from achieving unity as a human family, thereby leaving us prey to violence of all sorts.

Pope John XXIII hoped, through the missionary outreach of a united Church, to heal these very divisions. Both St. Augustine and the fathers of Vatican II believed that the Church could be the instrument not only for saving all peoples but also for uniting the world if the various churches and faith communities could heal their own internal disputes and external divisions.

St. Augustine delineated the *saeculum*, the world, as a theater for the contest between the sacred and the profane, between grace and sin. The communion of saints is entirely sacred and the collection of the damned entirely profane. The Church in the world is a mixture of wheat and weeds, but ever sacred in her Lord and in his gifts. The world, the *saeculum*, according to the Second Vatican Council, is loved by God; and the Church lives in the world as its leaven, promoting the sacred and combating the purely profane. St. Augustine and Vatican II teach a comparable vision of the relationship between Church and world because they have the same sense of mission from Jesus Christ: to unite the human race in the savior of the whole world.

A final observation about Augustine and the Catholic intellectual tradition: Cardinal Newman called St. Augustine the teacher who "has formed the intellect of Christian Europe."[19] From no one more than Augustine do we learn that teaching belongs to the very essence of the apostolate of the Church. Augustine not only wrote a catechesis for the young,[20] but his *Enchiridion* is one of the most famous catechisms in the Western Church.[21] Most important of all, he wrote a book specifically called *Teaching Christianity [De doctrina Christiana]*,[22] contain-

19. John Henry Newman, *Apologia pro vita sua* (New York: Longmans, 1908), 264.

20. Augustine, *The First Catechetical Instruction [De catechizandis rudibus]*, trans. Rev. Joseph P. Christopher (Westminster, Md.: Newman Bookshop, 1946).

21. Augustine, *The Augustine Catechism: The Enchiridion on Faith, Hope and Love*, trans. Bruce Harbert (Hyde Park, N.Y.: New City Press, 1999).

22. Augustine, *Teaching Christianity [De doctrina christiana]*, trans. Edmund Hill, OP (Hyde Park: New City Press, 1996). The translator defends the English title of this work in these words: "The one thing the work is not about is Christian doctrine. The word *doctrina* is not to be taken in the passive sense, which is the only one it has in English, for the matter taught, but in the active sense of the business of teaching....[Some even think] it presents us with a scheme for a Christian education, with what we might call Augustine's *Idea of a University*" (95).

ing the "first program of higher studies that provide a complete formation of the mind and are conceived solely in function of the religious purpose that Christianity assigns to the intellectual life."[23]

Pope Pius XI, in his Apostolic Exhortation of 1930, *Ad salutem humani generis*, expressed well the Church's esteem for her bishop and teacher:

We have retraced.... the life and merits of a man with whom one will not find another to compare, or certainly very few, from the beginning of the world to the present day, on account of the power of his penetrating genius, the sublimity of his holiness, and the victorious combat which he undertook to defend Catholic truth.... Surely no one is unaware of the admirable manner in which St. Augustine wrote of the divine government of all things and all events of history in his noble work on *The City of God*. For he made use of everything he drew from an assiduous studying of the Bible on the one hand, and from the fullness of the human culture of his day on the other hand, in order to produce one integrated concept of the history of the world.[24]

One integrated concept, not only of the relationship between faith and reason, but beyond that, one integrated concept of the history of the whole world: we,

23. Henri Marrou, *S. Agostino e la fine della cultura antica* (Milan: Jaca, 1987), 331.

24. Cited in Eugene Kevane, *Augustine the Educator: A Study in the Fundamentals of Christian Formation* (Westminster, Md.: Newman Press, 1964), vii.

in an age of globalization, can teach that the universal communion of the Catholic Church is the sacred counterpart of the secular solidarity of the human family because, in part at least, we ourselves learned this truth from St. Augustine.

CHAPTER 3

How God Thinks

THE *SAECULUM*, the area where the distinction between the profane and the sacred is played out, is the
theater for two conversations. The first, between faith
and culture, is important because both are ethically
normative systems and, if the norms of the culture di-
verge too greatly from the norms of the faith, then believers live in great tension and the culture is imperfect-
ly open to realities beyond itself. The second dialogue
that takes place in the *saeculum* is that between faith
and reason, because faith gives us revealed truths and
reason helps us to find what is true.

If there is tension between the truths of faith and
the truths that are in the canon of reason at any particular cultural moment, believers live in anxiety and
are tempted to a skepticism that closes in on itself and
is unworthy of human reason. Institutions that foster
conversation between faith and culture, which makes
rational norms available at a particular place and in a
particular time, and between faith and reason, which

has its own formal structure and is never totally captured by any particular culture, are important for culture, for faith, and for the people shaped by both.

The relationship between apostolicity, which is one of the four classical marks of the Church, and the teaching Magisterium of the bishops, begins with the recognition that both are carriers of the tradition that links us to Christ. Being Catholic means accepting tradition as a source of religious truth. Protestantism, by contrast, comes out of a religious stance that does not accept communal tradition as a normative source of knowledge about God. Where influential, it has helped to create cultures that reject tradition as normative for institutions or even for personal actions. That said, the rejection of tradition in favor of personal judgment does not necessarily entail individualism concerning how we come to know or how we judge our actions to be good or bad. A culture can be nontraditional, yet also tribal, to the extent that persons let themselves be guided unreflectively by choices and values of those who form the majority of the moment.

When she passes the midpoint of Lent, the Church in her liturgy reads from the Gospel according to John. She watches and hears Jesus moving from his preaching and his performing of miracles, healing the sick, walking on water, changing water into wine, to a more explicit claim to an identity with God, whom he calls his Father: the Father and I are one; God and I act together. This "Father" is the God of Abraham, Isaac, and Jacob, the one who, when Moses asked him in the presence of the burning bush, "Tell me who you are so that I can tell the Egyptians and my own people who sent me," replied, "I AM who am." That enigmatic phrase has occasioned a wide range of interpretations, from the oracular admonition that God is beyond human knowing to Aquinas's philosophical exposition of *ipsum esse subsistens*, God as pure existence. Notwithstanding the multiple layers of explanatory tradition attending the divine name, Jesus' use of "I AM" language in the Gospel according to St. John is a clear claim to divinity: "before Abraham came to be, I AM." The God of Abraham, whom we worship as the Father of our Lord Jesus Christ, is someone for whom all times are "now." There is in God's inner life no past or future. He is eternal. Human beings, being finite, live in time; time is one of our creaturely limitations. Yet we are also made in God's image and likeness, and thus we have a yearning for something beyond our own limitations, a foothold beyond this place, a desire for the eternal in the midst of time. How can we make the past present and normative for the future, so that past, present, and future come together in a way analogous to God's eternal simplicity?

In a traditional society, the past is still vital; it continues to influence, though not always determine, thought and behavior in the present. But what is past can shape lives now only if it transcends its own time, only if a mythical narrative erases the distinction between past and present. In speaking of art, literature, or philosophy, for example, we distinguish a "classic" work from a period piece in the recognition that there are works of imagination and intellection that point to truths beyond the local and temporal circumstances of their creation and thus are achievements of permanent human importance. In a popularly nontraditionalist society, however, where "history is bunk," people believe knowledge of the past is useless in understanding the present or preparing for the future: the past is to be left behind.

In a society that lives by the myth of progress, it is the future, not the past, that determines meanings and norms in the present. Consequently, planning becomes a crucially important enterprise; planning is a way of bringing the future into the present so as to shape us and change us now. We plan not according to the norms of the past but, rather, from what we have been brought to believe the future is calling us toward. Hence the "norms" proposed by our vision of the future no longer operate as axioms in our moral deliberation but are presented as facts — inevitable changes of circumstances — to which we will find it advantageous to adapt ourselves as quickly as possible. Progressivist societies accordingly speak of "the *demands* of the future."

The Catholic Church insists that faith brings us into God's perspective, God's vision of things, which is always *sub specie aeternitatis*, from the viewpoint of eternity. St. Paul claimed to have "the mind of Christ" long after Christ was crucified. The claim that we have the mind of Christ is possible only if Jesus of Nazareth was not captured by his own time and its own influence and continued as a causal agent after his death. People of faith acknowledge that Christ has risen from the dead and therefore forever escaped his own time and space. Those convictions are implicit in the Church's profession that Jesus is Lord.

Christianity is, first of all, a way of life, an encounter not with an idea but with a person, with the person who made the claim "I AM" — "I am the Way, the Truth, and the Life." After the sacramental encounter with the risen Christ in baptism and the reception of his life through grace, it is necessary to have access to the truths of God's self-revelation in the living Jesus in order to grow in the spiritual life. How can we have access to the events in which God has revealed himself so that they are present to us and remain normative for the future? How can we assure continued access to God's grace? The apostolicity of the Church, the community founded upon faith in Christ's resurrection, is our assurance of this access.

Theology of Apostolicity and the Church

St. Irenaeus, a second-century bishop of Lyons in what is now France, explained to both Catholics and heretics of his day what apostolicity means in terms that are now classic. He wrote, "Anyone who wishes to discern the truth may see in every church in the whole world the apostolic tradition clear and manifest.... This apostolic tradition has been brought down to us by a succession of bishops in the greatest, most ancient, well known Church, founded by the two most glorious apostles, Peter and Paul at Rome.... For with this Church, because of its more effective leadership, all Churches must agree, that is to say, the faithful of all places, because in it, the apostolic tradition has always been preserved."[1]

"Always" wasn't a particularly long time in the second century. Irenaeus was two generations removed from the apostles. But the seeds of a mature theology of apostolicity are already present in his work. Four of these truths are of particular importance. The first is that the apostle is a disciple. The office of an apostle is grounded in the initial call, "Follow me," that Jesus addressed to those whom he first summoned to accompany him in his ministry. This initial "follow me" applies

1. Irenaeus, *Adversus Haereses* III.3.1 and 3.3, cited in Matthew Lamb, "Vatican II after Fifty Years: The Virtual Council versus the Real Council," in *The Second Vatican Council: Celebrating Its Achievements and the Future*, edited by Gavin D'Costa and Emma Jane Harris (London: A. and C. Black, 2014), 12.

as well to all the successors of the apostles, since the same Lord promised, "I will be with you always until the end of the world."[2]

Professor Joseph Ratzinger — later Pope Benedict XVI — explained the interpersonal character of apostolic succession and tradition:

"Tradition" is never a simple, anonymous passing on of privileged ideas but is personal, is the living word, concretely realized in the faith. And "succession" is not a taking over of official powers, which then are at the disposal of their possessor, but is rather a dedication to the Word, an office of bearing witness to the treasure with which one has been entrusted. The office is superior to its holder, so that he is entirely overshadowed by that which he has received; he is, as it were — to adopt the image of Isaiah and John the Baptist — only a voice that renders the Word articulate in the world.[3]

So an apostle is a disciple first of all. It means he is profoundly involved with someone who first called him and whom he has come to recognize as Lord.

The second point about apostolicity is that the apostle therefore has an obligation to bear witness to the treasure of the living truth with which he has been entrusted. All baptized Christians, of course, have the office of witness: they can speak authentically from their

2. Mt 4:19; 9:9; 28:20; see Mk 1:17; 2:14; Lk 5:27; 24:48; Jn 1:43; 17:18–21.
3. Joseph Ratzinger, "Primacy, Episcopate and Apostolic Succession," in *The Episcopate and the Primacy*, by Karl Rahner and Joseph Ratzinger (New York: Herder, 1962), 37–63; the quotation is from 46–47.

personal experience of grace about who Christ is for them. The important difference of the apostolic office is that the successors of the apostles must speak about who Christ is for *everyone*. The apostle bears witness to who Christ is for the whole Church, and this office is always superior to its holder and to personal experience.

Speaking to the type of witnessing that transcends a sharing of personal experience, Joseph Ratzinger wrote, "if true apostolic succession is bound up with the Word, it cannot be bound up merely with a book, but must, as the succession of the Word, be a succession of preachers, which in turn cannot exist without a 'mission,' i.e., a personal continuity reaching back to the apostles.... Apostolic succession [in the Church] is the living presence of the Word in the person of witnesses. The unbroken continuity of witnesses follows from the nature of the Word as *auctoritas* [authority] and *viva vox* [a living voice]."[4]

But this Word, to be living both in the proclaimer and in the hearer, requires faith to be recognized and to be received. An authentic theology of apostolicity and its relationship to the Magisterium is possible only where faith enlightens reason. If the light of faith is extinguished or excluded, all that is left to connect today's believers with Jesus' apostles are texts — classic texts perhaps, norma-

4. Ibid. 53–54.

tive in some sense for some peculiar reason, but so many dead letters whose basic truth is never grasped.

Appeals to sacred texts fail if the texts themselves are severed from this living apostolic tradition of the Church's faith in and worship of her risen Lord. This severing often results from reliance on historical scholarship that rejects the testimony of faith on *a priori* grounds, such as those whose method has its origins in the *Theologico-Political Treatise* of the seventeenth-century Dutch philosopher Benedict de Spinoza. This methodological move underlies the third key to understanding the apostolic office. Since an apostle must witness not just to his own experience but to the fullness of truth, any textual scholarship that is divorced from the faith community that gives us the text's full meaning necessarily breaks historical continuity and prevents the text's serving as a source of understanding God's perspective operative in human history. The text does not carry the tradition that unites us to Christ.

Spinoza, in his classic treatise, identifies the power of nature with the voluntarist power of God. God and nature are the same, and Spinoza asserts that the proper method for interpreting Holy Scripture is the same as that used to interpret nature.[5] As with studies of nat-

5. Benedict de Spinoza, *A Theologico-Political Treatise; A Political Treatise* (Mineola, N.Y.: Dover, 2004), 45 and 99. On the importance of Spino-

ural phenomena, the first step is the methodological rejection of the idea that the Bible has a special unity that gives meaning to its parts; rather, the Bible is to be analyzed by breaking it up into discrete parts, whereby the meaning of one verse can only be determined by another verse, much as a laboratory researcher breaks up nature into distinct elemental parts in order to understand the operation of each. In such a system, only those meanings are to be accepted that anyone, including an unbeliever, could accept on purely empirical grounds.

A second methodic step is rejection of the "truth question." The verses of the Bible are not to be accepted as true when they refer to realities not perceptible to common human sense experience or to rational deduction. Just as Newtonian mechanics sought to explain only perceptible three-dimensional motions, so Spinoza's canons of interpretation recognize only those perceptible textual meanings found in the scriptures as a composite. For Spinoza, faith is not a lamp illuminating the mind but a blind act of piety and obedience. No theology founded on obedience to a supernatural revelation has power ever to oppose reason. In Spinoza's program of enlightenment, naturalist and secularist reason conclusively dethrones theology rooted in faith.

---

za for the Enlightenment, see Jonathan Israel, *The Radical Enlightenment: Philosophy and the Making of Modernity (1650–1750)* (Oxford: Oxford University Press, 2001).

His disciples therefore easily moved from empirical scholarship to an ideology of power: *true* religion is that which is natural and rational, whereas *revealed* religion "is merely a fraud and a political tool in the hands of Jewish, Catholic, or Protestant authorities."[6]

Recent popes have emphasized the responsibility to cultivate the wisdom traditions of philosophy and theology that are fundamental to Catholic intellectual life — for the sake both of the Church and of the global cultures in need of moral and religious direction. The question of truth in matters moral and religious has to be raised within the context of the quest for wisdom, goodness, holiness, both within the full ecclesial communion and in conjunction with all "people of good will." Truth cannot be consigned to a utilitarian toolbox, as it has been from the European Enlightenment onward, as if it were an instrument of social or civil dominative power. Both nature and history are ordered to ends inscribed in their very existence by their Creator and Redeemer. Both metaphysics and theology have suffered from the eclipse of wisdom in modern and postmodern cultures.

Imagine a historian who would attempt to write a history of mathematics without acquiring knowledge of the conceptual foundations and analytical opera-

6. See Israel, *Radical Enlightenment*, 654.

tions of mathematics. Such a historian might do a passable job of comparing various mathematical texts, of dating and locating them, of working out the cultural processes that were operating at the time the texts were produced. He could deduce who used which text to get what advantage in this or that situation, how such a text was a basis for concrete applications in engineering or commerce. Undoubtedly, such a history would be useful to those interested in the societies and institutions on which the progress of mathematics impinged. But no one could claim that such a work merited the name of a critical history of mathematics. Analogously, those who would attempt to expound the Christian religion, while having amputated that witness to faith that is its fullness, are doomed to focus on the superficial and peripheral at the expense of the essential. It was in recognition of this flaw that Cardinal Ratzinger wryly remarked, "Wherever theology ignores this subject — the Church — it turns into a philosophy of religion."[7]

The fourth point in elaborating the theology of apostolicity is the connection between the apostolic office, the mission that Christ gave the apostles, and the celebration of the Eucharist in the church. Drawing especially on Augustine, Thomas Aquinas situates apostolicity in the carrying forward in history of the visible

7. Ratzinger, *A New Song for the Lord: Faith in Christ and Liturgy* (New York: Crossroad Herder, 1997), 171.

and invisible missions of the Word Incarnate and the Holy Spirit. In Question 43 of the first part of the *Summa theologiae*, on the Divine Missions, Aquinas remarks on the mission of the Holy Spirit for the founding of the Church. He writes, "In a special sense, a mission of the Holy Spirit was directed to Christ, to the apostles, and to some of the early saints on whom the Church was in a way founded.... To the apostles the mission was directed in the form of breathing to show forth the power of their ministry in the dispensation of the sacraments; and hence it was said, 'Whose sins you shall forgive, they are forgiven' [Jn 20:23]; and again under the sign of fiery tongues to show forth the office of teaching; whence it is said that, 'they began to speak with divers tongues [Acts 2:4].'"[8]

Later, especially in his lectures on the Gospel according to St. John, Aquinas comments on the appearance of the risen Christ to the apostles. Jesus showed them the marks of his passion because the body that was crucified is truly risen but in a transformed state. Then he invests them with their office. This office or ministry is not something the apostles choose; it is laid upon them as a yoke (*iniungit officium*). It comes from God, not from their own will or choosing. "As the Father sent me, even so I send you," Jesus says. This is an office and

8. Thomas Aquinas, *ST* I, 43, 7, ad 6, ed. English Dominicans (New York: Benziger Brothers, 1911) (adapted).

mission laid upon them by Christ sending them into the world to continue his own mission from his heavenly Father.

St. Thomas remarks:

This shows that Christ is the mediator between God and man: "There is one mediator between God and men, the man Christ Jesus" (1 Tm 2:5) This was to console the disciples; acknowledging the authority of Christ, they knew he was sending them by divine authority. They were consoled that they were given a dignity, namely that they had the proper office (*officium*) of apostles, for an apostle is one who has been sent.[9]

Being sent as an apostle is hardly a dominative position. It reflects the wisdom and power of the Cross. Aquinas envisages the Lord, saying,

As the Father loving me sent me into the world to suffer for the salvation of the faithful — "For God sent his Son into the world, not to condemn the world but that the world might be saved through him" (Jn 3:17) — so I, loving you, send you to undergo suffering in my name — "I send you as sheep in the midst of wolves." (Mt 10:16)[10]

This apostolic participation in the salvific suffering of the Son is given when our Lord breathes upon the apostles as a visible sign of his sending the Holy Spirit. To be configured to the crucified Christ, the apostles

9. Aquinas, *Lectura super Evangelium S. Ioannis* (Rome: Marietti, 1952), XX.iv.n2537.
10. Ibid.

must be born again in the Holy Spirit. Aquinas talks about the similarity between the handing on of the Spirit to the apostles at the beginning of the Church and the breathing of life into man's nostrils in the book of Genesis. "Jesus makes them fit for the [apostolic] office by giving them the Holy Spirit, 'God enables us to be ministers of the New Testament [given] not in letters but in the Spirit' [2 Cor 3:6]. In this giving of the Spirit, he first gives them a sign of this gift, that is, 'he breathed on them.' There is something similar in Genesis [2:7] when God 'breathed into man's nostrils the breath of life,' when the first man "corrupted his natural life, but Christ has repaired this by giving the Holy Spirit."[11] The Lord's breathing is a visible sign of the invisible sending of the Holy Spirit. The risen Lord signifies by this breathing the extending of the Holy Spirit to the apostles for the sacramental mission of forgiveness and sanctification. Later, at Pentecost, the tongues of fire signify the Holy Spirit's mission for teaching and preaching. Bishops and priests are only instruments of Christ who gives eternal life and who teaches eternal truth.[12] Our understanding of the Holy Spirit is deepened when he is sent not only as the Spirit of Life, as in Genesis and other books of the First Covenant, but also as the Spirit of Truth, as in the books of the New.

11. Ibid., n2538.
12. Ibid., n2543; see also nn2538–44.

Our Lord founded the Church on the twelve apostles, who are the foundation stones of the new Israel, by sending them and by continuing to send their successors until he returns.[13] So Aquinas says, "The apostles and their successors are God's vicars in governing the Church that is built on faith and the sacraments of faith. Wherefore, just as they may not institute another Church, so neither may they deliver another faith, nor institute other sacraments: on the contrary, the Church is said to be built up with the sacraments 'which flowed from the side of Christ while hanging on the Cross.'"[14]

For Aquinas, neither the apostolic succession nor the sacraments can be understood apart from the mission received by the apostles from the risen Lord. It is mistaken to imagine that Aquinas's confidence in the ongoing apostolic tradition in the Church results from a deficiency of historical-critical scholarship. While this scholarship may give us a more detailed knowledge of manuscript and other textual details, the truth of the reality referenced by the texts can only be properly understood and known by the signs of faith.[15] The Church as

13. On the succession of the apostles and the Petrine ministry, see Hans Urs von Balthasar, *Explorations in Theology*, vol. 4, *The Glory of the Lord*, and vol.7, *Paul Struggles with His Congregation*; and Ratzinger, "Primacy, Episcopate and Apostolic Succession," 37–63.

14. Aquinas, *ST* III, 64, 2, ad 3.

15. Avery Dulles, *The Catholicity of the Church* (Oxford: Oxford University Press, 1985), 68–146; see also von Balthasar, *The Moment of Christian Witness* (San Francisco: Ignatius Press, 1969).

a living presence of the Divine Word mediated by apostolic succession and carried forward in history again depends upon the missions of the Son and the Holy Spirit and is sacramentally embodied in the Eucharist. The Church confects the Eucharist and the Eucharist creates the Church, and in the Eucharistic action the apostolic nature of the Church is truly made visible.

It is within sacramental worship — members and head visibly present through the sacraments of Baptism and Holy Orders — that apostolicity can be eminently understood as fulfilling the Word Incarnate's promise to be with the Church until the end of time and to keep God's people in the truth. Holy Scripture is read in the liturgy because the Church is a community of faith. The Church at worship is the context for interpreting the text of scripture. She is the living community of faith that gives the texts their proper understanding by relating them to the realities of faith through the tradition that binds us to Christ. This tradition is made visible in the governance of bishops in union with the Bishop of Rome, having power from Christ to sanctify and teach the truth of Christ's Gospel. The act of faith doesn't end in the statements of the creed and Church dogmas; it attains the sacred realities themselves.[16] We don't worship

16. See Aquinas, *ST* II-II, 1, 2, ad 2: "the act of the believer does not reach its end in a statement, but in the thing: we do not form statements except so that we may have apprehension of things through them; as in knowing, so in faith."

and pray to concepts, symbols, and propositions; we worship and pray to and believe in the Father, Son, and Holy Spirit. A genuine theology of the Church's Magisterium therefore places it in the service of the truths revealed by the triune God, who created the entire universe and has redeemed mankind through the mission of the Word Incarnate and the Holy Spirit.

Theology of Magisterium in the Church

Apostolicity means that the Church conserves and transmits, through the office of bishop, the truths of divine revelation, the content of our faith. The Magisterium, as it relates to that conservation, is the guarantor. If one makes truth claims about our life with God as disciples of Jesus Christ, why and how can one give a guarantee for those truth claims? Cardinal Newman, in his essay on the development of doctrine, puts it this way: "Surely, either an objective revelation has not been given, or it has been provided with means for impressing its objectiveness on the world. If Christianity be a social religion, as it certainly is, and if it be based on certain ideas acknowledged as divine, or a creed (which shall here be assumed), and if these ideas have various aspects, and make distinct impressions on different minds, and issue in consequence in a multiplicity of developments, true, false or mixed, as it has been shown, what power will suffice to meet and to do justice to these conflicting conditions but a supreme authority ruling and reconciling individual judgments by a divine right and a recognized wisdom.... there can be no combination [of various dogmas] on the basis of truth without an organ of truth."[17] If apostolicity is the conserver of truth, there must be some organ that guarantees that the apostolic office teaches the truth in every age.

Newman goes on to speak of the way in which doctrinal accountability guarantees the truth that comes to us in apostolic tradition. In a less ecumenically sensitive age, he wrote, "By the Church of England a hollow uniformity is preferred to an infallible chair; and by the sects of England an interminable division. Germany and Geneva began with persecution and have ended in skepticism. The doctrine of infallibility is a less violent hypothesis than this sacrifice either of faith or charity. It secures the object while it gives definiteness and force to the matter of Revelation."[18] So the Magisterium, the organ of the bishops' teaching office, is at the service of the truth that is transmitted and preserved by apostolicity.

The theological basis for the Magisterium can be found in two exchanges in Holy Scripture. The first passage that one should reflect on when one hears the word

17. John Henry Newman, *An Essay on the Development of Christian Doctrine* (London: Basil Montagu Pickering, 1878), 89–90.
18. Ibid., 90–91.

"Magisterium" is the dialogue between Jesus and the apostles at Caesarea Philippi, recounted in chapter 16 of Matthew's Gospel. In that narrative, Jesus was teaching, preaching, and working miracles, and people were saying various things about him. Jesus turned to the twelve and said, "Who do people say that I am?" They responded with the terms that their culture gave them. "You are John the Baptist." They knew John the Baptist. "You are Elijah." They knew Elijah. Then Jesus said, "Who do you say that I am?" Peter spoke up and said, "You are the Christ, the Son of the Living God." Then Jesus responded, you're right, but you didn't learn this from your own experience. You know because the Father has revealed it to you, and so now I'll tell you, Simon, who *you* are. You are Peter. That exchange dovetails with the account given in the sixth chapter of the Gospel according to St. John; after Jesus proclaims that the Bread of Life is not just something he gives, but something he *is*, many of the disciples turned away. Jesus asked the twelve, "Will you also go away?" They said, "To whom shall we go? You have the words of Eternal Life."

It is noteworthy that in both of these instances it is the Lord who begins the conversation. He is the one who puts the questions, "Who do you say that I am?" "Will you also leave me?" The authority of the apostles is not self-started. It doesn't take the initiative; it is elicited by Jesus' raising the question. It is the Lord who first questions his Church — sometimes indirectly through the arrangements of his providence — and all deliverances or statements of the Magisterium answer to this prior and foundational elicitation of the witness that Christ himself calls for.

In both Gospel texts, the authority of the teaching office is granted in the address of Jesus himself. Whenever any one of us questions an interlocutor in a genuine dialogue, we empower him to answer. In our questioning, we help to make him capable of speaking an answering word. The question that Jesus posed to the apostles presupposes they can answer, although in this case the basis of that testimony to the truth about who Jesus is is not something purely and entirely human.

But we have to go further. The Lord starts the dialogue, and the Lord gives the power to respond, to teach the truth about who he is, to say to the world who he is. Because of who Jesus is, the apostles must answer. The Lord's question is not just an invitation to answer but rather a demand to tell him who they think he is and then to tell the world. The Lord's question in Matthew 16 lays on the apostles the requirement to proclaim the Christological faith that Peter articulates. Similarly, in the sixth chapter of John's Gospel, when Jesus asks, "Will you also leave me?" he is asking, "Will you, who are keeping my company, also keep faith as I deliver myself in the Eucharist to the Church, by which acts I include in my identity as the Christ all Christians, making them members of my Body by giving them my flesh and blood?" In both cases, the urgency of St. Paul's exclamation is anticipated: "Woe to me if I do not preach the Gospel" (1 Cor 9:16). The encounter in the sixth chapter of St. John serves to complete the commission recorded in Matthew. Jesus is the Christ, the Son of the living God, who is also truly present in the Eucharist under the species of bread and wine; we become Christ's body not just in our profession of faith but in our reception of the sacraments.

From what was said above, then, it is clear that the Gospel demands a magisterial witness that is Christological in the fullest sense. Christ is the anointed one; included in his office and in his person are all who are baptized in water and the Spirit. The Eucharistic confession in John 6 is not an addition to the confession of Matthew 16. "You are the Son of God" is fulfilled in the Eucharistic celebration of Christ's disciples. There is a coinherence of Christological and Eucharistic doctrine.

Just as it was in the breaking of the bread that the risen Jesus was made known to the disciples at Emmaus, so St. Irenaeus argues for the doctrine of Incarnation on the basis of the Eucharistic practice of the Catholic Church. He writes, "When, therefore, the mingled cup and the bread made by hands receives the Word of God, and the Eucharist of the Blood and the Body of Christ is made, from which things the substance of our flesh is increased and supported, how can [anyone] affirm that the flesh is incapable of receiving the gift of God, which is life eternal. . . . even as St. Paul declares in his Epistle to the Ephesians [5:30], that 'we are members of His body, of His flesh, and of His bones.'"[19] Pope John Paul II took great care to clarify and corroborate Catholic moral teaching by displaying its Christological foundation — a foundation that has become obscure for many Christians, for whom the profession of faith about who Jesus is was entirely distinct from the demands of Christian discipleship, particularly those demands belonging to the Church's moral doctrine. By a parallel effort, the precepts of the natural law have in recent years been explored by means of the contemplation of Christ in his virtues. This is a pastoral dimension of the exposition of natural law, which presupposes a rational, philosophical justification, but transforms it in the light of faith.

As magisterial teaching is always, at root, Christological, so too it is always scriptural. Peter answers Jesus, "You are the Christ," employing the words and categories of scripture. So also the recognition of Jesus as the Bread of Life, though rejected as a shocking departure from tradition by many who first heard the claim,

19. Irenaeus, *Adversus Haereses* V.2., in *The Ante-Nicene Fathers*, edited by Alexander Roberts, James Donaldson, and A. Cleveland Coxe (Grand Rapids, Mich.: W. B. Eerdmans, 1981), 1:528.

is adumbrated by the teachings of Exodus 16 and the book of Proverbs. This tethering of the Magisterium to scripture is effected by the Lord himself when, in Luke 24, he explains to his disciples on the road to Emmaus and to the apostles waiting in Jerusalem everything that concerns him in the law and the prophets and the psalms. "It was ordained that the Christ should suffer," and it took the word of God Incarnate to break open for them this revelation from the scriptures they thought they understood. The apostolicity of the Magisterium brings it about that the light of understanding the scriptures given to his chosen witnesses by Christ should be preserved in the Church throughout her history by that "organ of truth" that Newman insisted was necessary to authentic discipleship.

Magisterial teaching, moreover, shares the sacramental structure of the apostolic office as a whole. In other words, the Magisterium makes present something that is much more than the teaching and more than the words in which the teaching is given. In bestowing on the apostles the authority to teach, Jesus gives them a share in his self-dispossession. Jesus doesn't speak in his own name. "The teaching is not my own — it is from the one who sent me." He tells the apostles, "I cannot do anything on my own" (Jn 5:19). He is a sacrament of God and of God's will for the salvation of the world. Everything he has to say is from the Father, so Christ in his self-dispossession is transparent in such a way that through him the Father himself is present. It is in his selflessness that Christ's supreme authority is seen. The apostles, *qua* apostles, have only what has been given them; like Jesus, they have nothing of their own.

There is a parallelism between the mission of Christ and the mission of the apostles. Jesus gives the apostles a participation in his power and the authority to speak in his name. He confers on them an office that replicates the shape of his own mission: "Whoever receives you receives me, and whoever receives me receives the one who sent me" (Mt 10:40; Jn 13:20). In all this, it is clear that the words of human beings are *capax verbi Domini*; the words of human beings are capable of expressing the word of the Lord. This is important to emphasize because, were it not the case that the word of the Lord can get into *our* words so as to be repeated in praise and confession of the Lord, then neither the Church, nor Holy Scripture, nor the apostolic office itself could be a reliable vehicle of divine truth.

In the light of faith, there is no separation of an unfulfilled dogmatic intention from an always inadequate and culturally contingent conceptual expression, as if an apostle can only aim at the reality he speaks of but cannot declare the truth of it. To affirm that dogmatic formulae "adequately express" the divine realities they convey does not mean that everything that can be said is communicated in them. It does mean, however, that what has been said is truly said and tells us reliably about divine reality, and not just our relationship to it.[20] It is true that we will not know what the Bread of Life is until the full display of the Paschal mystery, until we see God face to face and know as we are known. Even so, once the Lord himself has taken up the prior words spoken by Moses and the prophets, and once he has reshaped them on the anvil of his passion and death, by that fact they truly become adequate channels of his truth. The apostles, through their participation in the Lord's own life, in his passion, death, and resurrection, are similarly reshaped. The Lord said that if you are going to tell the world who I am, you must share in my passion. That is the promise. Magisterial teaching is, consequently, always Paschal. The authority given the apostles in Matthew 16 and 18, before Christ's passion, is fulfilled after the resurrection in John 20: "Receive the Holy Spirit; whose sins you forgive, they are forgiven." John shows that this commissioning of Peter and the apostles occurs only once the Spirit is given, the Spirit who will recall for them all the teachings of Jesus (Jn 14) and who will guide them into all truth (Jn 16).

Apostolicity is a spiritual endowment, and the apos-

20. See on this point the Congregation for the Doctrine of the Faith, *Mysterium ecclesiae* (June 24, 1973), and Paul VI, *Mysterium fidei* (September 3, 1965), nos. 24 and 25.

tles' ability to confess Jesus as Lord is strictly a function of their own redemption by the grace of Christ and their sharing in the Spirit with which he is anointed. That the Spirit is an interior condition of the possibility of magisterial authority is indicated already at both Caesarea Philippi and Capernaum. For it is not flesh and blood that has revealed to the apostles that Jesus is the Christ, the Son of the living God, but the Father. And no one believes in Christ unless the Father draws him (Jn 6:46, 6:65). It is because the apostles are so illumined and so drawn interiorly by the Holy Spirit that they know who Jesus is and do not depart with the others, knowing also that Jesus alone has the words of everlasting life.

It must also be acknowledged that, at Caesarea Philippi and Capernaum, it is Peter who gives voice to the apostolic group: "Peter spoke enthusiastically and authoritatively on behalf of all [the Twelve]," Pope Benedict reminds us.[21] Peter's role as spokesman is enabled by the requirement that he give blood witness to Christ's own shedding of his blood. This is signified at Caesarea Philippi by the transformation of Peter's name; it is signified in the Gospel according to St. John by Jesus' threefold commission to feed his sheep — when the Lord indicates to Peter "by what death he

21. Benedict XVI, Angelus Address at Castel Gondolfo, August 24, 2008.

was about to die" — contrasting with his threefold denial that he ever knew Jesus. The interpersonal character of magisterial authority is evident in Peter's relation to Christ and to all the apostles together. This is something of a disputed point in the theology of the Magisterium, where we meet two subjects of magisterial authority inadequately distinguished: Peter in his personal charism and Peter and the other apostles together. It is always true that Peter cannot be understood apart from his being at the center of his fellow apostles; but neither do the apostles form the group they do without Peter. He can speak for them and they can speak through him. This mutually exercised charism is clearest in the ecumenical councils, but the collegial relationships are found analogously also in synods and episcopal conferences.

We must reckon finally with the fact that magisterial witness — both at Caesarea Philippi and Capernaum — is projected eschatologically: that is to say, in view of the end and consummation of all time. The apostles do not depart from their Lord at Capernaum because, as Peter said, his words are the words of everlasting, eschatological life. For his part, at Caesarea Philippi the Lord says that what Peter binds on earth is bound eschatologically, in heaven. This means that the magisterial office and its acts have the enormous responsibility of guiding the growth of the pilgrim Church through all the ages to her eternal destiny. In that sense, the apostolic office participates in the contemporaneity of God's own perspective. Magisterial teaching and apostolic witness give us all hope that we will see the Lord face to face. *In patria*, restored to our true and final home, we shall need no apostolic words because we will be in the presence of the Word made flesh. We shall need no sacraments because we will be seated at the wedding feast of the Lamb.

Here again we can learn from St. Irenaeus: "The path of those belonging to the Church circumscribes the whole world, as possessing the sure Tradition from the apostles, and gives unto us to see that the faith of all is one and the same, since all receive one and the same God the Father, and believe in the same dispensation regarding the Incarnation of the Son of God, and are cognizant of the same gift of the Spirit, and are conversant with the same commandments, and preserve the same form of ecclesiastical constitution, and expect the same advent of the Lord, and await the same salvation of the complete man, that is, of the soul and body. And undoubtedly the preaching of the Church is true and steadfast, in which one and the same way of salvation is shown throughout the whole world, for to her is entrusted the light of God."[22]

We have reviewed very quickly some distinguishing characteristics of the magisterial office, which is entire-

22. Irenaeus, *Adversus Haereses* V.20., 1:548.

ly at the service of the apostolic tradition that unites us to Christ and guarantees the Church's mark of apostolicity. We have seen again how the truth of the Magisterium is bound up with the life of discipleship. The spiritual life of an intellectual presupposes immersion in the Catholic intellectual tradition. Let me note now cultural problems we often have in receiving these gifts of apostolicity and its guarantor in the Magisterium of the Church today.

Presently, we live our faith in the circumstances of a widespread societal conviction that truth claims in religion are inherently dangerous. There is also a more vague but diffuse fear that, if there is a Lord, we are in danger of losing our autonomy. In our individualistic culture, personal autonomy is perhaps the primary value accorded the human person. Authentic religion provokes suspicion and alarm because it demands conversion, a change, the forfeiture of our self-sufficiency to a relationship that is not of our making and the commitment to an encounter of which we are not the master.

That is another fear embodied in our culture today: the fear of the Church's claims about herself as well as her claims about the Lord, for her claims about Jesus and herself are universal and immutable. She claims that the mission the Spirit gives the Church comes from God's will, his will that the whole world come to know Jesus Christ and worship him as one fold gathered around one Shepherd. This claim rejects religious pluralism as an ideal and so threatens widely held convictions about the absolute primacy of freedom and about what conditions of freedom are indispensable. There are powerful societal forces opposed to the theology of apostolicity and thus many places where the truth claims made by an apostolic Church and guaranteed by the Magisterium are neither persuasive nor acceptable.

Yet the Magisterium is always at the service of apostolicity, and apostolicity is at the service of the truths given us by God in divine revelation, claims that make demands upon us if we are to live a spiritual life. Jesus promised that "The truth shall make you free," but where objective truth is regarded as the enemy of human liberty, many will abandon truth even though they ultimately forfeit liberty as a consequence, for we can't be free if cut off from the truth of things. To live in falsehood is to live beneath human dignity, in the space where any emancipation is meaningless. That confronts us with the most culturally outrageous statement that can be made in our time; but it is true: The Church is where you go when you want to be free.

CHAPTER 4

A Christian Intellectual in a Post-Christian Society

OUR SENSE OF WHAT IT MEANS to be free in public life in modern times was set forth in the Treaty of Westphalia in 1648. In the German city of Cologne, there's a small church right next to the famous cathedral. The church's chapel is dedicated to St. Stephen and is under the pastoral care of the Dominican friars. It houses the tomb of St. Albert the Great. Albert was not originally buried there, and when they moved his body from its former grave, they opened his casket and found still-very-well-preserved vestments, most of his crozier, and his bones. Being able to touch the palpable relics of St. Albert is particularly significant in that the friar, as well as being the teacher of St. Thomas Aquinas, was an empiricist. As an empiricist, Albert had an approach to study and to life that began with the senses, not *a priori* with ideas, but rather with what we see, feel, and touch. It is quite literally a down-to-earth approach to knowing, although influenced by the Augustinian and

Platonic ideas that had shaped the Church's main intellectual tradition for many centuries.

Albert was an empiricist, but he wasn't a secularist. He began his thinking with what was in front of him, with what he could discover using empirical methods, but his way of thinking, his approach to life, was not without explicit and public reference to God, faith, and religion. In contradistinction to secular*ism* — an atheistic position that excludes God explicitly as an impermissible hypothesis — secularity may be understood as the pursuit of human activity without any explicit or public reference to God or to a religious belief.

This notion of the secular is based upon a distinction that faith itself admits, and in fact insists upon, between faith and the *saeculum*, the world. But the distinction can be made in either a friendly way or a hostile way. It can be proposed so that the integrity of the world and that of faith are each preserved, or it can be made in such a way that one pole of the dichotomy threatens the other. St. Albert's calling as a Catholic scholar was to be part of an intellectual tradition that started with the recognition that faith and world are truly distinct, but nonetheless not antagonistic.

St. Albert's own calling to explore that tradition and to advance it as a Catholic scholar and saint was in a nonsecular context, of course. He was a citizen of a Christian commonwealth. He belonged to a newly formed religious community, the Order of Preachers, that revivified biblical studies and did so in a context of personal and community life marked by evangelical poverty. He belonged to a diocesan church as its bishop, and he was on the faculty of nascent universities, that is, the successors to the cathedral schools, to the mendicant *studia generalia*, and, before that, to the monastic schools, which led to the formation of the first universities in Bologna, Oxford, and Paris. It was St. Benedict's foundation of monasticism in the West that enabled oases of learning to survive together with worship of God in the center of life when civil structures were collapsing during the so-called Dark Ages. These institutions, the monastic institutions and the schools that were part of them, were able to keep learning alive in an unsettled, sometimes anarchic epoch. But by Albert's time, social institutions had emerged from a new and robust Christian culture. The Renaissance of the eleventh and twelfth centuries was in full flower and took place, moreover, within a society and via a form of learning that was not secular. Being on the other side of an Enlightenment that sees faith and world as unfriendly, today's scholars use the terms "secular" and "nonsecular" with a different tone than did St. Albert. In exploring the history of that change of meaning, we approach an understanding of the task of the Catholic scholar in a post-Christian society and can recognize again how the intellectual life and the spiritual life, each respectful of the other, strengthen each other.

For descriptive purposes, we can say that a Catholic scholar is someone who self-consciously contributes to an intellectual tradition that relates faith to reason while doing justice to both, that makes explicit the desire to keep them in conversation in such a way that one can learn from the other. Starting at the very beginning, this is a tradition that goes back to the apostles themselves, who had to figure out how they could continue to be monotheists as Jewish believers and still affirm that Jesus Christ is God. Of course, even the partial elaboration of Christology and of trinitarian theology took some centuries to achieve. Yet even the first generation, the apostolic fathers, had to depart at times from the vocabulary of apostolic preaching and of scripture itself, borrowing conceptual tools from the pagan philosophers and scientists and transforming them in service of a new form of learning that was genuine on its own terms, logically coherent and faithful to its canons of evidence, and at the same time authentically Christian. That process began with St. Paul himself, who expounded the truths of our faith while thinking self-consciously in conformity with the strictures of human logic.

The tradition was developed in the apologists of the second century. St. Justin the Martyr, who was trained in pagan philosophy and rhetoric, wanted to recast the faith as a philosophy. He called Christianity a philosophy, the science of the times, a love of truth that shaped a way of life. That's how he defended himself when called before the tribunal that eventually decreed his execution. He talked about a philosophy that was true as opposed to all other philosophies, which were false. St. Justin related faith to philosophy by applying faith as a touchstone to philosophical assertions, making distinctions within philosophy itself between that which prepares the way for faith — and is thus obviously true — and that which isn't consistent with the faith — and is therefore an intellectual dead end.

Beginning the conversation concerning what we can know by revelation and what we discover in the world through our own experience, we asserted that the preeminent figure in the Western intellectual tradition is St. Augustine of Hippo. As previously discussed, faith and reason are, for Augustine, parallel to one another, though dialectically related. He was a Platonist, and he used that dialectic method to explore how *a priori* ideas that seemed to be inconsistent with one another could still be kept together in justified tension. It was only at the end of the patristic period, with the beginnings of Scholasticism, that the goal became not just to hold faith and reason in tension but to integrate them. This integrative impetus came strongly into the Catholic intellectual tradition with Scholastic philosophy and, most particularly, in theology, in the great tradition of the university commentaries on the *Sentences* of Peter Lombard. In his own *Summa theologiae*, St. Thomas Aquinas showed how faith and reason might be put into a conversation in which one learns from the other. Integration of faith and reason, of the whole of our knowledge with the whole of our faith, is the goal and the mark of a Catholic scholar. The aim is to live with *all* the truths that God wants us to know: those truths he has revealed and those truths he wants us to discover. Most importantly, the goal is to live with God Himself as a saint.

There are, of course, different ways of positioning faith and reason. Among the Jewish traditions, for example, is a movement called modern orthodoxy, for which the paradigm might be found at Yeshiva University in New York. Yeshiva University is *de facto* two universities. On one part of the campus, scholars wearing yarmulkes grapple with scripture. Students continue a rabbinic tradition of debating difficult passages in the Torah, the Law, in an ongoing dialectic with a fellow student kept as a partner for the full length of the program. In the afternoon, after seven daily hours of intense engagement and debate, the same students leave their sacred texts and *mishnot* and move into what is a completely modern university, the same as any other modern university, with various undergraduate and graduate departments, research programs, and fully accredited medical, graduate, and professional schools. The students pursue these programs side by side with their study of Torah. There is no attempt to bring the two together. That kind of consciously unresolved equilibrium is not part of the Catholic intellectual tradition; it can result in secularism on the one side and fideism on the other. The Catholic scholar works from a personal conviction that, tensions and difficulties notwithstanding, a believer's calling to the intellectual life cannot be ultimately at cross purposes with the profession of the Catholic faith. The life of reason, pursued with earnestness and integrity, deepens the life of faith; the life of faith, conducted with authentic devotion, enriches the life of reason.

That's the calling; then there's the context. Albert the Great's context was Christian. Ours is not, at least not in the same way. Where the notion of faith or that of reason is deficient or incomplete, the project of putting the two of them into a positive relation with one another can be challenged or opposed. In pagan Rome, Justin Martyr's claim that true philosophy was none other than Christian faith put him in collision with the religion of the state. In the culture of a contemporary secular university, faith and reason are not only distinct but, in the minds of many, unable to enter into conversation. They cannot be related, let alone integrated.

There are several reasons for this attitude. One is

the difficulty that the various disciplines have relating to one another. A scholar is rewarded in a university by advancing knowledge, and, for all but the most brilliantly creative few, knowledge is advanced by specialization. Interdisciplinary work is hard. The type of synthesis that demands a polymath's knowledge eludes us as specialization burrows more and more deeply into *minutiae* and leaves less time for synthesis. So the very project of a Catholic scholar is not something that the structure of a university, as presently constituted, would nourish because the university today rarely advances projects of intellectual synthesis. Related to this difficulty is the widespread structural incoherence, a disciplinary Balkanization, that vexes the integrity of the academic curriculum and, in truth, turns the meaning of the word "university" into an anachronism. In his book *Beyond the Culture Wars*, Gerald Graff wrote, "An undergraduate tells of an art history course in which the instructor observed one day, 'As we now know, the idea that knowledge can be objective is a positivist myth that has been exploded by postmodern thought.' It so happens that the student is concurrently enrolled in a political science course, in which the instructor speaks confidently about the objectivity of his discipline as if objectivity had not been exploded at all. 'What do you do?' the student is asked. 'What else can I do?' he says, 'I trash objectivity in art history and I presuppose objectivity in political science.' To some the moral of such a story would be that students have become cynical relativists who care less about convictions than about grades and careers. In fact, what is surprising is that more students do not behave in this cynical fashion, for the established curriculum encourages it."[1]

The disjunction of the curriculum is a far more powerful source of relativism than any doctrine preached by any member of the faculty. As Pope John Paul II taught in his 1998 encyclical letter *Fides et ratio*, relativism is corrosive not only of faith but of reason itself; that said, the context of the secular academy works to penalize religious conviction, or at least religious profession, disproportionately to its institutionalized academic disciplines. Whence the pope admonished us, "[One of the tasks that Christian thought will have to take up is] the segmentation of knowledge with a splintered approach to truth and the consequent fragmentation of meaning [that] keeps people today from coming to an interior unity."[2] We're at war not only with one another. We're at war within ourselves.

This brings us to a second difficulty: the fact that the secular university continues the Enlightenment ideology whereby faith and reason were viewed as inimical to

1. Gerald Graff, *Beyond the Culture Wars: How Teaching the Conflicts Can Revitalize American Education* (New York: W. W. Norton, 1992), 105–6.
2. John Paul II, *Fides et ratio* (1998), 85.

one another. The great myths of the modern intellectual tradition, beginning with the trial of Galileo, portray the faith as opposed to science, and therefore to research and to the intellectual life. In this view, religion may perhaps be tolerated as a source of personal comfort or ritually enacted solidarity, but neither the life of faith nor even theology has anything important to *teach* the university — or indeed any of the citizens of the world of reason.

How have Christians responded to this divorce of faith from reason, divine Word from real world? One can examine the university as an arena of the disciplines and look then at the intellectual influence of faith on them, or one can look at the academy as a particular subculture that has its own way of being human and that welcomes or repels the Church and the community of faith. Christian scholars and theologians have devised different methodologies to pursue this question.

On the left is the classical correlation position, with its roots in Schleiermacher and Heidegger and given fullest expression more recently by Paul Tillich — the correlational position between faith and world, faith and culture. Here philosophy examines the culture and surfaces the anxious and unresolved questions of being; and theology, inspired by the revelation of scripture, provides the answers of being itself. The theologian's task is then to correlate questions and answers, respecting both sides of the equation. In the 1960s the World

Council of Churches propounded as one of its slogans "to meet the world's agenda," without asking whether we meet it on the world's terms or rather provide something unattainable by the world for the sake of the world itself. Karl Barth ruefully commented that such a method would work in paradise but not in our sinful human condition: we are characterized by sin and fallen in mind, we are incapable of raising the right questions, and therefore our answers are always skewed. It was not until the coming of Christ that we even knew how to stammer out the right questions of finitude.

A more nuanced critique is offered by the University of Chicago's David Tracy. While respecting the intuitions of correlation, he nonetheless finds the method "crucially flawed." Tracy thinks it naïve to hold that philosophy and cultural analysis simply raise questions that come humbly to the court of theology for resolution. It is clear that, from the pre-Socratic thinker Parmenides on, philosophy has provided plenty of answers to its own questions — at least until late in our own day, when it has become almost exclusively a critical discipline or metadiscipline without its own vision. Thus authentic correlation must involve a more subtle play between the questions and answers of the culture on the one hand and the questions and answers of the theological and biblical tradition on the other. It is here that Father Tracy turns to Gadamer and Ricoeur and their hermeneutic of a "fusion of horizons." The Christian interpreter, the systematic and fundamental theologian, comes to a classic text of Christianity, to a saint, a narrative, a work of art, and the like, and allows the world of that Christian text to mix with the world, with questions and convictions of his or her culture.[3]

The Yale school, led by George Lindbeck and Hans Frei, critiques even the nuanced correlational approach of a David Tracy. With his roots theologically in Barth and philosophically in Wittgenstein, Professor Lindbeck proposes that the Christian Church is a self-contained and self-regulating community, without a necessary relationship to anything else, bound together and organized according to a particular set of linguistic rules or language games, which, of course, are always cultural games, as well. The theologian's task is not to attempt a dialogue with the language games of the culture, since that usually results in a distortion or watering down of the distinctiveness of the Christian way of being in the world. Rather it is to clarify the grammar of Christian discourse, showing how rules of theological speech both flow from and reinforce uniquely Christian praxis or discipleship.[4]

More recently, Kathryn Tanner attempts an inter-

3. David Tracy, *The Analogical Imagination: Christian Theology and the Culture of Pluralism* (New York: Crossroad, 1998).

4. George Lindbeck, *The Nature of Doctrine: Religion and Theology in a Postliberal Age* (Philadelphia: Westminster, 1984).

esting simultaneous criticism of both correlation and the postliberalism of Lindbeck.[5] Both the correlationists and the followers of Lindbeck share a common assumption that Christianity is a self-contained and easily described totality, much like the tribes and cultures naively examined by the anthropologists of the early twentieth century. To be sure, the correlationists and the postliberals propose doing very different things with Christianity: the first, putting it into some sort of dialogue with the secular culture; the second, analyzing its linguistic and behavioral distinctiveness. But they come together in overlooking the fact that Christianity has never been and never will be culturally isolated. Tanner argues that Christianity has always taken shape on the border between itself and secularity, usually sharing much of the same content as the secular culture but giving that content a unique value and orientation. For her it is not so much what Christianity has but how it has it that matters. Thus Paul accepts much of Greek culture; Augustine embraces much of the Roman world; Thomas Aquinas takes in Aristotle, but each Christian views the cultural content uniquely and distinctively.

Another departure from both correlation and postliberalism is the Christian phenomenology of Jean-Luc

5. Kathryn Tanner, *Theories of Culture: A New Agenda for Theology* (Minneapolis: Fortress, 1997).

Marion. A nostalgic postmodern, as he calls himself, Marion proposes a fundamental theology that is not so much a dialogue with a skeptical culture as a phenomenology of the Christian's holding up of the icon of Jesus. Because he accepts the Heideggerian critique of metaphysics, he does not move to anything more substantive than what phenomenology alone will permit. One can add the substance later on in a roundabout way, as he does in *Dieu sans l'être*.[6] Like Barth, von Balthasar, and the postliberals, Marion seems to think that the dialogue has led more often than not to a watering down of the alluring power of Christian truth. The Christian fundamental theologian walks around the Christian fact much as the phenomenologist walks around a physical or psychological object, allowing its facets and profiles to emerge and then engaging it in clarifying description. And that is not bad, but for the fact that one must walk around it with the world in one's hand, bracketed in that way, or else something goes seriously wrong in the life of discipleship and the life of faith.

Moving more boldly to the right, we find the neo-Augustinianism of John Milbank.[7] In the tradition of Christopher Dawson, Milbank argues that much of modern social theory and philosophy represents a fall-

6. Jean-Luc Marion, *God Without Being* (Chicago: University of Chicago Press, 1991).
7. John Milbank, *Theology and Social Theory* (Oxford: Blackwell, 1992).

ing away from an integral Christian vision of the whole. Thus Hegel's philosophy of Spirit is a truncated and secularized account of providence, called reason; the myth of progress is a psychologized account of divinization through grace; and Marx's philosophy of history is a politicized version of Christian apocalypticism. That is a well-worked-out thesis by Milbank, but not new. All of modern philosophy can be explained, if you like, in an overarching thesis that, until this generation, we have taken all the prerogatives of the Divine Mind expounded in medieval theology and put them into human reason in philosophy. The pathetic mistake of all liberal theology for Milbank is the establishment of dialogues between the satisfying and holistic Christian account of reality and what amounts to heretical distortions of that account. In that sense it is easier to dialogue with Aristotle as a pre-Christian than with Hegel. Milbank's view is that Christianity itself, with its ontology of creation, its praxis of forgiving love and nonviolence, its theology of a God who graciously pours himself out, constitutes a distinctive way of being in the world, but not of the world. In *The City of God*, Augustine refused a dialogue with what he saw as an essentially corrupt Roman polity. Rather, he proposed the fact of Christianity as a rival and an opponent to it. Most Christian theorists from Thomas Aquinas to H. Richard Niebuhr to Gustavo Gutierrez have, according to Milbank, departed tragically from this Augustinian boldness and have tried to come to terms with the city of man.

In these multiple efforts to accord human reason and Christian faith their due respect we may find variants of the approaches of Justin Martyr and Augustine and Aquinas: different views of how all mankind has been damaged by sin (and the redeemed healed from it), different degrees of confidence in human nature (and of the effects of grace upon it), consequently different views of which "direction of influence" has been beneficial, if indeed possible at all.

The Sociological Dimension: The Crisis of Liberal Catholicism

We can now move from the theological to the sociological dimension of the distinction between Church and world and between faith and culturally programmed reason. Ironically, in view of the aim of Vatican II's pastoral constitution *Gaudium et spes* (1965) that the Church bring her own unity and healing to a divided *saeculum*, a source of consternation arises when all the divisions of the culture along liberal and conservative lines come into the household of the faith.[8] Some years ago, in a talk to the National Association of the

8. Vatican II, *Gaudium et Spes*, in *The Documents of Vatican II*, edited by Walter M. Abbott, 299 (New York: Guild Press, 1966).

Laity, I said that we are at a turning point in the life of the Church in this country and that liberal Catholicism is an exhausted project. By that I meant that liberal Catholicism is a victim of its own success. The liberal critique has been turned inward; it is not a critique of society, which is now largely a liberal project, so much as a critique of the Church, which is slow in accepting the presuppositions of populist liberalism. After having journeyed around the world visiting missionaries for twelve years, one of the strangest phenomena I found coming back to this country was a resistance to seeing the faith as a source of freedom. In country after country, culture after culture, place after place, the space, if there was any, of freedom and of hope was very often carved out by the Church, usually in very difficult circumstances — sometimes politically oppressive, often economically oppressive in the midst of poverty, sometimes culturally benighted. When I came back to this culture, I realized that the critique that had been part of liberationist thinking in this country was turned primarily internally on the Church herself, as if she were the source of oppression, benightedness, and poverty.

The answer, however, to this exhaustion of liberal Catholicism is not to be found in a type of conservative Catholicism so sectarian in its outlook that it cannot serve as a sign of unity of all peoples in Christ: a sacrament of the unity of the human race. The answer is simply Catholicism in all its fullness and depth; the faith able to distinguish itself from any culture, and yet able to engage and transform them all; a faith joyful in all the gifts Christ wants to give us, and open to the whole world he died to save. The difficulty arises when the Church speaks of her own authority, which in many minds is quickly equated with "control," intellectually and socially. Many of the Catholics of my own generation found, after the Council in particular, a liberating moment in their own life through secularity. Secularity suddenly opened up horizons that had not been theirs in a Church that, rightly or wrongly, was judged stifling.

Paradoxically, people get stuck in their liberating moments. We recognize a clear distinction between people for whom secularity is liberating because faith was too closely bound up with externalities that no longer gave life, and those who have grown up in a very secular milieu and do not find secularity at all liberating. They find it a prison; they find it closed in upon itself. There is no openness to transcendence. Gasping for air, they turn to the faith for freedom. When both sorts of Catholics — some students, some professors — find themselves in a secular university, they may strive with equal ardor to integrate the life of faith and that of reason, but they will locate their confidence and wariness in different traditions, different institutions, different systems of reward and punishment.

So what can be said about the duties of the Catholic academic *tout court*, regardless of background, training, or circumstance? A Catholic needs three things to maintain an academic vocation with integrity as a calling, a way of discipleship grounded in faith. First of all, he must be competent as a scholar. There are professional standards that have their *raisons d'être*. A scholar, particularly one with a university appointment, must carry on research, publish, and teach at different levels, must advise students, must fulfill responsibilities for the university, must enter into the politics of the university in order to protect his own discipline and contribute through it to the advancement of learning. That is to say, competence includes the willingness to create and maintain a community of scholars. The scholar needs to respect obvious canons of civility in every discipline and have a capacity for friendship. An academic has to be able to interact with students, to dialogue with peers, to contribute something personally — besides professional expertise — to a community of scholarship. The scholar comes with expertise paid for through a lot of hard work. Competence isn't just for graduate school; it's for professional schools, for engineering, for medicine. All of them have their own standards that have to be met if one is to be accepted as a scholar at all.

The second thing necessary for integrity as a Catholic intellectual in a secular university is to be a serious disciple of Jesus Christ in his body, the Church. His faith need not always be made public, but it should be practiced — and not in secret. The sacramental life of the Church is part of one's life. One does works of charity, tries to promote a more just social order, conforms one's personal moral life to the teaching of Christ and the Church. One's personal habits leave room for a time for prayer, communion, and conversation with the Lord. One should be familiar, to some extent, with scripture and how to approach it in an intellectually honest way; the symbol system of the faith and the scriptural world enter into the scholar's mindset so that his mental world is more profound than that of politics and his own discipline.

Though not absolutely necessary, it is eminently consistent with being a serious disciple of Jesus Christ for a scholar to have a sense of and respect for the entire Catholic intellectual tradition. Such was not the organizing idea of the American scholar in Emerson's famous essay *Self-Reliance*, which claimed you start with yourself and discard all traditions in order to think freely and rely only upon your own experience. For a while, people applauded that project, but true scholars know it is illusory. We don't ever create things solely from our own experience. Emerson failed to see that because of his quasi-mystical belief that the self was truly universal. He maintained that we are each part of an over-soul, so to be one's self is by that very fact to be universal. But the fact is we have to rely upon tradition — language itself being a prime example — even in the act of creatively departing from that tradition. This applies to any human enterprise, whether intellectual, social, or pragmatic. If you don't know the history, you can't know where you can go.

A Catholic scholar, no matter what his discipline, should also have some sense of the intellectual tradition that has shaped the conversation between faith and reason in his own area of study. A Catholic scholar should relate his intellectual life not only to the faith, as lived and used for personal integration, but also as an intellectual enterprise that opens up realms of intellectual exploration. This conversation keeps shifting. Even in the hard sciences, the faith has interesting things to say. Cosmology is again coming into its own; a larger perspective about the natural universe is now being re-conceptualized. The scientists who most truculently contest the faith today tend to be biologists rather than physicists, even though for more than a century physics seemed to be the prime antagonist of faith in God. All that has been transformed now because good physics has recognized it needs a context larger than the natural order in order to explain itself to itself.

The integration of faith and reason, and of faith life with intellectual life, demands a certain internal discipline. Both faith and the intellectual life train one to be attentive; faith and prayer bring one to be attentive to God and to the movements of the Spirit in one's own soul; intellectual discipline makes one attentive to the reality being studied, so that one can make new connections between apparently disparate phenomena and notice departures from the illusory patterns maintained by convention and sloth. "God is in the details," as Mies van der Rohe used to say about architecture. But God is in the details in every discipline, and so the habit of attention that is part of one's intellectual life is also a habit useful in one's faith life. The habit of attention necessary for study is very useful in giving time to prayer. The final test of whether we are serious about being a disciple of Jesus Christ in the Church as a scholar is to look at how we spend our time. One cannot live as a disciple without spending time every day in prayer, conversation with the Lord, just as one has to spend time each day with one's own discipline in order to be professionally competent. Attention and time are part of both callings, and they come together when we ask ourselves concretely, "how do I spend the time God has given me?"

The final element necessary to a Catholic scholar in a secular context is to be part of the self-consciously Catholic community. No one goes to the Lord alone, and no one is a scholar alone. If one is going to do both, then within the secular academic community there must be some parallel coming together of the Catholic community in order to support intellectual life. Focal points can be found within a secular university that is only warily and sporadically open to Catholic thought. Sometimes there is a Catholic chair, sometimes a mixed chair of religion that includes Catholic studies, sometimes an informal reading group of scholars studying a Catholic author. The history of the Church tells us of people who were introduced to the Catholic intellectual tradition, even informally in a secular context, and have then suddenly discovered their calling to be a Catholic scholar.

We might reframe the problem of integration of faith and reason as reflection on *mission*: in the eyes of the Church, what is the Catholic scholar *sent* to accomplish? The Second Vatican Council affirmed the Church's mission as an integrator, an organ of unity. This purpose is spelled out in Pope St. John XXIII's apostolic constitution *Humanae salutis* (December 25, 1961), in which he convoked the Second Vatican Council. Vatican II was to be a missionary Council, and the dogmatic constitution *Lumen gentium* therefore defined the Church as "the sacrament.... of the unity of the human race" — the visible sign that safeguards invisible ecclesial communion.[9] Since the whole human race is called to be visibly one, ecumenism, interfaith dia-

9. Vatican II, *Lumen Gentium*, in Abbott, *Documents of Vatican II*, 1.

logue, the development of all the concentric circles that Paul VI set out in *Ecclesiam suam* (1964), are to keep the Church moving outward in dialogue in order, finally, to unify both the Church and the world.

The same mandate, the same mission, is given to Catholic scholars in a way keeping with their vocation, to unify knowledge and faith as much as they possibly can, to take responsibility for integrating knowledge and faith and then responsibility for the public conversation, which must remain open to everyone's perspective so that it remains civil.

The abandonment of this search for an intellectual synthesis over the past two centuries has had social consequences. In the last two hundred years, our public life in the West has been much more dominated by will than controlled by reason. We've largely given up the search for an integration of knowledge, as particular specializations result in control, in dominance, but not necessarily in greater insight. If a society believes that it is possible to come to a rational synthesis of some sort, both in one's own vision of things and in our way of living together, in our moral code, then there are some intrinsic limits to behavior. But when that interior rational control disappears, the human project is then subject only to power, to will, and to willfulness.

In the search for rational norms for human conduct that are necessary to live together in peace, we can't be content with truth for you and truth for me, with truth in science and truth in scripture. Our very nature as rational beings impels us to keep trying to see how everything relates — deep calls unto deep (Ps 42:7) — how all truths hold together. The springtime of unity, coherence, peace that St. John XXIII thought would come from the Second Vatican Council falters without Catholic intellectuals doing the hard work, the disciplined work that is entailed in accepting a calling to be a competent intellectual and to be a disciple of Jesus Christ in the Church. Doing this in order that the public conversation will be rational and open to faith and will be a way to make peace puts us on a mission to help create a very different world than the one we live in right now.

CHAPTER 5

A Christian Intellectual and the Moral Life

IT IS COMMONPLACE to note that, since the years of the Second Vatican Council, our world has changed culturally, morally, politically, ecclesiastically. At the close of the Council, there was not a single country outside the totalitarian world in which abortion on demand was licit. The great ideological battles of the time took place between the still vigorous Communist world and the Western democracies. Soviet premier Khrushchev threatened in 1956 that the economic machine of the Soviet Union would "bury" the West — and many Western intellectuals continued to believe that the Marxist-Leninist organization of the state offered the best hope for producing just social conditions, the sacrifice of human freedoms notwithstanding. The Cuban missile crisis had only recently occurred; the Vietnam War was just beginning to heat up. The ramifications of the great social dislocations of the 1960s, which would bring with them the sexual revolution and its cognate assault on the family, were still without clear form. The historian Philip Gleason has spoken of this period as "the perfect storm" of cultural change that would leave no human institutions untouched.[1] The Catholic university was no exception.

Three features of Catholic higher education in the contemporary environment will structure the observations that follow. Two of them are quite well known and have been much discussed for some years now; the third, perhaps, needs to be examined more carefully than it usually is. These issues are (1) the increasing secularization of Christian higher education over the last century; (2) significant changes in Catholic moral theology and moral philosophy; and (3) the rise of secular moral philosophy in the applied ethics revolution that began in the 1970s.

The Secularization of Catholic Universities

The secularizing trend in Christian higher education began within the Protestant world of higher education at the end of the nineteenth century and then engulfed the world of Catholic higher education in the years after the Second Vatican Council. Two enterprises splintered Protestant denominations themselves and worked to secularize the universities: confrontation with Darwin's

1. Professor Gleason made this remark in a unpublished talk given at the University of Notre Dame in October 2005.

theory of evolution and the use of the historical-critical method as the authoritative means of understanding the Bible. Since direct access to Holy Scripture was central to Protestant self-definition, when the underpinnings of sacred scripture were attacked, the Protestant denominations divided into more liberal and more fundamentalist factions, and the universities sponsored by what became the liberal denominations eventually secularized themselves. Throughout the nineteenth century, the president at most Protestant universities was often a clergyman or at least a philosopher of a vaguely Platonist persuasion and therefore someone who could give ethical instruction to the students so as to provide them with an intellectual basis for moral living. That tradition of presidential pastoring disappeared as the disciplines became more professionalized and as the universities, one by one, severed their relationship with the founding denominations.

Studies of this phenomenon by Protestant scholars like George Marsden and Mark Noll, as well as those by Catholic scholars like Philip Gleason and James Burtchaell, have provoked a debate about the nature and extent of this secularization as well as about the factors that contributed to it.[2]

2. James Tunstead Burtchaell, CSC, *The Dying of the Light* (Grand Rapids, Mich.: W. E. Eerdmans, 1998); George M. Marsden, *The Outrageous Idea of Catholic Scholarship* (Oxford: Oxford University Press, 1997); Philip

For Catholics reflecting on the impact of this secularization, the controlling document must be Pope John Paul II's *Ex corde ecclesiae* (1990). This apostolic constitution emphasizes the historical emergence of the Catholic university from "the heart of the Church," developing a number of proposals for enhancing the Catholic character of contemporary universities. This document was met with some alarm at many Catholic colleges and universities when it was first promulgated. It was deemed acceptable as a roster of ideals, but when it set out specifics and became a set of regulations backed up by canon law, there surfaced the concern for how Catholic universities in the United States could remain joined to the American tradition of academic freedom. Some feared that the document presaged the intention of the bishops to interfere with the autonomy appropriate to the particular disciplines and to the university as a whole.

A pressing problem for those Catholic universities trying to resist secularizing forces is how to recruit and maintain faculties in which a significant number of the professors are convinced Catholics. Catholic universities have grown enormously in recent decades, in size, wealth, and academic ambition. It is only natural that these universities would want to use their advantages

---

Gleason, *Contending with Modernity: Catholic Higher Education in the Twentieth Century* (New York: Oxford University Press, 1995).

to enter the circle of elite institutions of higher education. It goes without saying that, in order to take its place among the distinguished research universities, a Catholic university should find it necessary to hire faculty members from those graduate programs that have already reached the highest levels of academic distinction. This dynamic of hiring, however, makes it difficult for a Catholic university to maintain a faculty that is predominantly or significantly Catholic. But for Catholic parents who send their children to Catholic universities, it is difficult to understand how a university can be genuinely Catholic unless a central core of faculty members practice the Catholic faith, and these misgivings find an echo in *Ex corde ecclesiae*.

A number of strategies, of different degrees of promise, it seems to me, have been proposed to deal with this problem. The richest and arguably the most academically distinguished Catholic university in the country has recently inaugurated a program to identify leading Catholic scholars at all stages along the continuum of academic development, from graduate students to distinguished chaired professors. The program was initiated in response to the precipitous drop in the percentage of self-identified Catholics on the faculty. A faculty that in the 1960s was well over 90 percent Catholic had become a faculty with a very slim majority of Catholic members. The administrator who directs this program is specially charged with ensuring that those who make academic hiring decisions at the university are aware of possible Catholic candidates. He has, however, no special authority to compel those making the hiring decisions to hire the Catholic candidates he has identified, particularly in research departments. It is the department that knows its own discipline and is responsible primarily to the discipline itself and not directly to the university that makes the final decision on hiring. In short, being Catholic is treated as an affirmative action category on the same level as being a woman or belonging to certain ethnic minorities.

Other Catholic universities and colleges have adopted the strategy of pooling their Catholic faculty resources in a single department, program, or college. The proliferation in recent years of Catholic studies programs at Catholic colleges and universities is evidence of the frequency with which this strategy is pursued. Many have worried that these programs, by focusing on the Catholic character of some part of the college or university, give implicit permission for the other parts of the university to forsake even the appearance of Catholic character. These specialized programs also seem to run contrary to the deeply Catholic idea that it is the Catholicity of the university as such — and especially as carried by the theology department — that provides the unifying structure of the university. As discussed in the previous chapter, it seems perversely counter-Catholic that the Catholic distinctiveness of a community of learning should be quarantined in an isolated part of the institution rather than embodied in the whole.

These Catholic studies programs are nevertheless often very effective. This move makes good sense at a state research university. It makes less sense in the context of a Catholic university, but it can be useful even there, especially in a university already largely secularized. An even more radical approach to preserving Catholic character is to lodge it in some nonacademic part of the university. One might focus on the religious life in the residence halls or in campus ministry, the administration, or volunteer service projects. Surely a Catholic university will want to keep a Catholic presence in administration and student life, yet that by itself is not sufficient, for the university has as its goal the discovery and dissemination of truth. While a well-ordered life in the residence halls or a spiritually rich campus ministry program contributes in important ways to the university, it cannot replace the pursuit of truth as such.

The heart of the university is in the persons who carry out its teaching and research, who are figures that give the university its character and have preeminent influence in the lives of the students. Faculty set the tone for a university, and no amount of Catholic influence in administration or in campus ministry can supplant their influence. As every university administrator knows, an unsympathetic faculty can frustrate even the most carefully developed administrative plan, and faculty can take the university in directions the administration deeply opposes. It is difficult to imagine how a university could be in any significant sense Catholic if its faculty is dominated by those hostile to the Catholic intellectual tradition and its moral demands.

Likewise, volunteer service projects for students cannot of themselves make up for a deficiency in Catholic conviction, instruction, and controlling institutional vision. On the one hand, neither the Catholic Church nor the Christian and Jewish communities in a broader sense have a monopoly on loving concern for others; on the other hand, ideologies of social and economic reform have mutated into the most nightmarish totalitarian social experiments, destructive of human life and human dignity. Concern for the disadvantaged is a necessary, but not a sufficient, condition for Catholic identity.

Significant Changes in Catholic Moral Theology and Moral Philosophy

Recent years have seen a significant shift in the methodology of many Catholic moral theologians and moral philosophers in examining the foundational questions in ethics. For the first half of the twentieth century, the prevailing methodology for Catholic moral theology was guided by a broadly Thomistic natural law approach, in conversation with biblical "data." This conversation was rule-shaped and did not escape the charge of moral legalism or casuistry. The change in Catholic higher education brought about by the encyclical *Aeterni Patris* (1879) of Pope Leo XIII was marked by the use of scholasticism to revitalize the intellectual tradition of the Church, and the revival of neo-Scholastic philosophy dominated Catholic moral theology during this period. Although there were significant disagreements among those who worked within this tradition, there was a commonality of approach and framework. The work of such giants as Jacques Maritain and Yves Simon not only set the tone for the teaching of moral theology and moral philosophy at Catholic universities but also had a broader impact, an influence that was manifest in Maritain's role in writing and defending the United Nations Charter of Human Rights. Maritain's philosophy also underpinned the discussion on human dignity and freedom in the Second Vatican Council.

While it would be untrue to say that the natural law approach to moral and political issues was repudiated at the Second Vatican Council or that it ceased to be influential after the Council, there is no doubt that the Catholic world after 1965 gave these methods less central roles in ethical pedagogy than was the case previously. The Council documents invited more pluralism in moral theology and theology in general and severed the connection between a particular method of doing philosophy and the methods of Catholic theology. This development opened the door to approaches to moral theology and moral philosophy rooted in perspectives that earlier in the century would have been associated with the intellectual peril called modernism. There was also an emphasis in the conciliar documents on more scripturally based approaches to moral reflection that seemed to downplay traditional Thomism. The subjectivity that modernism interprets as subjectivism was captured in St. Thomas's presentation of the virtuous life; and virtue, especially the virtue of charity, became the form and framework for decision making in Christian morality.

The impact of these changes on the teaching of ethics at Catholic universities was evident in the staffing of ethics courses, the textbooks used, and in the theoretical approaches taken to ethical issues. While most Catholic colleges and universities continued to require some philosophy and theology courses, the Thomistic textbooks that had earlier structured the courses were replaced by texts drawn from the secular academy. Increasingly, faculty in the theology and philosophy departments of Catholic universities had their training in secular graduate programs, where the prevailing methodologies and orientation bore little relation to the Catholic moral tradition. Although many of the progressive doctrines in the tradition of Catholic social teaching were countenanced at these non-Catholic graduate schools, the foundational principles employed in secular departments in support of those doctrines bore little similarity to those enunciated in the Catholic social encyclicals.

The Rise of Secular Moral Philosophy in Applied Ethics

A third arena of change that is key to our discussion remains to be addressed: the shift in applied ethics. Along with changes in Catholic higher education and in Catholic moral theology and philosophy, there has also been a revolution in the last half-century in the role that the academic discussion of ethics plays in liberal democratic cultures, especially in the English-speaking nations.

The Australian moral philosopher Peter Singer holds a distinguished chair in ethics at Princeton University, from which he speaks as the world's most influential advocate of the moral legitimacy of infanticide, abortion, euthanasia, and other counter-Christian positions. He first came to public notice when he wrote an article for the *New York Times Magazine* entitled, "Philosophers Back on the Job."[3] Singer remarked that for fifty-some

3. Peter Singer, "Philosophers Back on the Job," *New York Times Magazine*, October 14, 1974.

years philosophers had been concerned with methodologies and foundations and did not imagine they could move on to applications, to applied ethics. They were now beginning to move back into that field in order to give moral guidance on bioethics and in many other fields that were coming into their own. Singer lamented the passive role academic moral philosophy had played throughout most of the twentieth century in the great moral controversies of that time. He blamed this passivity on the positivist restrictions on normative ethical thought that had hamstrung academic ethics throughout the first half of the twentieth century under the influence of Anglophone analytic philosophy and its severe self-limitations.

Moral philosophers in the analytic tradition had for most of this period confined their investigations to technical issues about, for example, the semantics of moral language and narrowly epistemological considerations in ethics. These "meta-ethical" investigations were conformed to the canons of what was called "moral neutrality" — this is to say, it was a methodological requirement of philosophy that it remain neutral with regard to any substantive normative considerations. Philosophy might clarify the foundations and methods of moral discourse, but it could not give conclusions. Moral philosophers had thus been methodologically barred from contributing to substantive moral debates during this period.

Moral philosophers gave almost universal assent to the principle that no moral values could be derived from purely factual claims, that one can't move from an "is" to an "ought." The classical philosophers had a way of using metaphysics to get from what "is" to what "ought" to be. But once analytic philosophy did away with metaphysics, moral philosophy had to limit itself to methodological clarification of moral statements, and moral philosophers also forbade other academics — such as social or natural scientists — from weighing in on substantive normative debates, lest they be guilty of the naturalistic fallacy, confusing what is with what ought to be.

Singer was surely right to lament the absence of secular moral philosophers from the great moral debates of our time.[4] His article, however, was hopeful about the future of moral philosophy in that he argued that the period of philosophical quiescence in normative ethics was coming to an end. He celebrated the publication two years earlier of John Rawls's book *A Theory of Justice*, probably the single most influential book on moral philosophy of its generation. It departed from the confining world of the "meta-ethical" and attempted a restoration of a moral philosophy aimed at developing a comprehensive normative theory that would provide

4. Nevertheless, his cultural myopia was clear in his failure to be aware that there had been a thriving tradition of neo-Scholastic moral philosophy that had vigorously engaged cultural questions throughout the first half of the twentieth century.

a justification of basic moral principles and undergird the practices of liberal democratic culture. While Singer the utilitarian disagreed with Rawls's particular deontological or neo-Kantian theory, whereby ethical duties might be derived from a self-ratifying exercise of reason, he nonetheless applauded Rawls's philosophical ambition in attempting to put in place a secular philosophical system that could provide a framework for rational discussion and resolution of the moral dilemmas of contemporary culture.

Singer correctly judged that Rawls's theory of justice marked a change in the methodology of twentieth-century academics; but after Rawls there was no more unity than before. Academic philosophers succeeded in obtaining significant authority in contemporary moral debates. Since the 1970s, applied ethics has become a significant factor in both philosophy and theology departments. Before that time it was unusual to find courses in philosophy departments on medical ethics, business ethics, environmental ethics, applied ethics of any sort. With Rawls, all that changes. Philosophy departments rushed to include courses in all the major applied areas — especially medical ethics and business ethics and, to a lesser extent, environmental and feminist ethics. There was a flood of new textbooks in these various areas and an increasing number of research centers focusing on applied ethics. Now virtually every large university has applied ethics courses and at least one ethics center. The number of journals in applied ethics has also grown rapidly, so that today there are many more articles published in applied ethics than on ethics in general. Ethicists, as they came to be called, assumed consulting roles on hospital ethics committees, served on national ethics advisory committees such as the President's Advisory Council on Bioethics, and spoke authoritatively in the media on moral issues of public concern. Ethical commentary has become so fashionable that even the *New York Times* initiated a column, "The Ethicist," to give its readers authoritative advice on matters of everyday concern.

Perhaps the most discussed instance of secular academic moral philosophers using their authority to weigh in on a matter of public concern was the publication in the *New York Review of Books* of a lengthy defense of the legalization of physician-assisted suicide. It was entitled "The Philosopher's Brief" and was written by a small group of America's most distinguished moral philosophers, including John Rawls himself.[5] This article appeared in 1997, in the weeks leading up to the Supreme Court's deliberations on the constitutionality of two appellate decisions (by the Second and Ninth cir-

5. Ronald Dworkin et al., "Assisted Suicide: The Philosophers' Brief," *New York Review of Books*, March 27 1997, http://www.nybooks.com/articles/archives/1997/mar/27/assisted-suicide-the-philosophers-brief/.

cuit courts) that had found a constitutional right to physician-assisted suicide. "The Philosopher's Brief" advised the court that there were sound moral and constitutional grounds — based in considerations of personal liberty and autonomy — to uphold these decisions. The Supreme Court overturned the two appellate decisions by a unanimous vote, though there is no doubt that the "brief" appearing over the name of respected and prominent American ethical philosophers had a significant impact on the public discussion of the issue.

This issue is gathering force in the public debate, particularly in the states on the West and East coasts of the country, those with the most secularized popular cultures. It was debated in Washington State while I was bishop there. It was defeated there, but has since been passed by popular referendum. It is also protected in law in a number of other states. What stops it from being a morally and legally acceptable form of killing? The argument that continues over the force of personal autonomy is not directly derived from any principle but, in the American political fashion, from a community who came forward who would be threatened by this newfound right to kill people weakened by disease. The disabilities community, particularly those who were part of an organization called "Not Dead Yet," people in wheelchairs, people with degenerative diseases, people who know that the quality of their life according to many standards is not very high but nonetheless do not want to live under a societal death threat, gave voice to a public appeal that was effective. Not only in Nazi Germany, but in every society that decrees that some of its members have a "life not worthy of living," ways are found to execute those deemed unfit. With testing for fetal abnormality now commonplace in the United States, at least 85 percent of those diagnosed with Down syndrome are killed before they are born. The eugenics movement is very much with us, but physician-assisted suicide has been at least temporarily derailed because an organized community stepped forward, helped by the fact that it is not a religious community. In a secularized society, religious people are counted out on the grounds that one can't impose *religious* views on another, even if the religious views have a rational foundation. If it's a religious person who makes it, a moral argument is deemed religious, even if its reasoning is purely philosophical.

One might suppose that secular academic moral philosophers are able to speak authoritatively on the deep moral disputes in our culture because they have reached a consensus, grounded in reason itself, on the foundational principles in ethics and their justification. But this hasn't happened. Their authority, purportedly, is the authority of reason itself, but one rational position contradicts another rational position. The publication of Rawls's *A Theory of Justice*, which is based upon Kantian ethics, was countered by the publication of a number of defenses of classical utilitarianism, where one argues from the consequences of actions or from values whose protection is advantageous. Later, new versions of Aristotelian normative theories were put forward — Alasdair MacIntyre's masterful *After Virtue* is a prime example — defending an ethics based on human happiness.[6] Academic moral philosophy was transformed almost overnight from a discipline in which applied ethics was sterile into a discipline in which it was almost overly fertile; one might say there were too many theories to make sense of them all. If one is an academically trained ethicist confronted with a concrete moral dilemma, how is one to proceed? Does one appeal to Rawls's Kantian foundational principles to settle the issues, to the utilitarian foundational principles of a pragmatic culture, or does one rather appeal to an account of the virtues as was elaborated by Alasdair MacIntyre, Martha Nussbaum, and many other philosophers who start not with a moral judgment of a particular act but with the moral demands of a "good life" as such?

The deep disagreement among secular academic

6. Alastair MacIntyre, *After Virtue: A Study in Moral Theory,* 3d. ed. (Notre Dame, Ind.: University of Notre Dame Press, 2007. (First edition published by Gerald Duckworth, London, 1981, and first U.S. edition, University of Notre Dame Press, 1981.)

ethicists at the foundational level makes it impossible to claim that there is any consensus among moral philosophers on how we should live or on how we should respond to the moral quandaries presented today. One might wonder why it is important for a philosopher to take up these questions if there is no agreement about them. These profound foundational disagreements among secular moral philosophers have, as it happens, led to the development of a certain style of textbook, as well as a standard kind of teaching technique, in many applied ethics courses. Since the contemporary student of applied ethics is confronted with a diverse group of foundational ethical theories that give different answers to concrete moral problems (applied ethics), textbooks tend to be structured so that students first explore the different kinds of theories and then examine the different answers they might give to practical questions.

Textbooks of applied ethics typically consist of an anthology of articles exploring different responses to the basic problems in an area like medical ethics. The articles will be divided into sections defined by different problems. In medical ethics texts, the main divisions might organize the articles into those having to do with matters of life and death in medicine, those having to do with doctor-patient relations, and those having to do with the justice of the health care delivery system itself. Preceding the articles on these particular issues is typically a presentation of normative theories in which the deontological, consequentialist, or virtue-based approaches are examined. There may also be a discussion about disputed foundational axioms, such as the principle of double effect. The student is invited first to examine the differences between the normative approaches and then asked to explore these differences by seeing how they yield different conclusions with regard to the concrete moral problems to be dealt with later in the book. This approach is, I maintain, the outcome of the predominance of case law theory in legal education.

From the time of Oliver Wendell Holmes, the academic instruction of lawyers largely gave up on principles, even the so-called common law principles, and moved into a theory of education predicated on cases. Lawyers reference precedent, but only as applied to a particular case. In the operation of this method there are no principles in general legal theory that would permit a lawyer to settle a case from deductive reasoning. For Americans, law is the most important cultural influence in our society; with our religious differences, our linguistic and cultural differences, it is law that unites us. As a consequence of our reverence for the law, the method of legal instruction that began at the end of the nineteenth century has moved now into the method of teaching ethics — case by case to case.

Some have thought that the presentation of multiple methodological foundations in teaching ethics is more likely to breed skepticism than to develop sensitive precision in responding to moral complexity. What seems clear is that it helps students see the deep moral disagreements in our culture; whether or not it helps them form characters that will let them navigate these difficult moral issues is harder to discover.

Alasdair MacIntyre has parodied this approach to applied ethics by suggesting that what philosophers actually do typically is to take difficult moral issues and, by careful analysis that traces conflict back to its roots in fundamental theoretical disagreements, demonstrate that these issues are not *difficult* to resolve but in fact *impossible* to resolve. The upshot, of course, is that we have to resolve them politically, through will and through majority consent.

The fact that there is no consensus among rationalist moral philosophers about foundational principles has not prevented them from claiming authority in public debate. One consequence of the lack of consensus is that the most formal and least contentful values take center stage. The value of patient autonomy referred to earlier has become the dominant value within contemporary medical ethics. Thus, when we are unclear on whether we are benefiting a patient by continuing life-sustaining care at the end of life, we leave the matter up to the patient. Or again, since the broader culture is unable to reach an agreement on the worth and dignity of fetal life, we resolve the problem by leaving it up to the choice of the pregnant woman. This resort to personal choice, put forward as a neutral and liberating value, has been responsible for some of the greatest atrocities committed in modern medicine. The frequency with which it is appealed to as the "value of last resort" in so much of secular academic ethics is testimony to the bankruptcy of this approach. Preserving Catholic health care institutions — which are still the only medical institutions in this culture where no one is deliberately put to death — is important not only because they serve the sick but also because they bear witness to values elsewhere abandoned.

Catholic Universities and the Moral Life

To return to the larger question: how should the contemporary Catholic university respond in both teaching and research to the great moral and cultural debates of our time? How can it operate as a moral agent, able to use the Catholic intellectual tradition in ethics and moral theology in order to guide believers in making decisions that keep them close to God? The last chapter of Philip Gleason's magisterial examination of Catholic higher education in the twentieth century, *Contending with Modernity*, is titled "The End of an Era." He tells the story in great detail of how Catholic universities in the twentieth century faced and surmounted the challenge to modernize themselves institutionally so that they could compete on the best of terms with secular institutions of higher learning. The loss in the 1960s of the intellectual framework that defined them, however, has provoked an identity crisis that still persists. His is not a recommendation that we return to the past in the attempt to recover depth and meaning. This would be impossible even if desired. Rather, Gleason suggests that we draw on the rich resources of the Catholic intellectual tradition to fashion a vision adequate to contemporary challenges but true to the moral and intellectual richness of that tradition itself. The concluding sentence of his book reads, "The task facing Catholic academics today is to forge from the philosophical and theological resources uncovered in the past half-century a vision that will provide what neo-Scholasticism did for so many years — a theoretical rationale for the existence of Catholic colleges and universities as a distinctive element in American higher education."[7]

These resources include, first of all, the doctrines of the Second Vatican Council, which addressed so many contemporary cultural issues; second, the ethical teachings of the recent popes, which provide key ideas for criticizing much of secular applied ethics; third, the

7. Gleason, *Contending with Modernity*, 322.

comprehensive statements of Catholic social teaching in the Catechism; and fourth, the continuing stream of encyclicals and other documents that comprise Catholic social teaching. These documents have proven that they have the capacity to instruct and to inspire and could thus be part of a force that could focus and teach on moral matters in the contemporary Catholic university.

In a sense, Professor Gleason is calling for something like the labor schools that existed in the 1930s under Catholic auspices, which were far more radical in their principles than anything in American intellectual life in their own time and in ours. Catholic social teaching provided a quite radical critique of American capitalism and was, for that reason, not very well thought of outside of Catholic circles. With the increased academic suspicion of papal teaching authority after the Council, these and other encyclicals ceased to be an academic resource, to the great detriment of intellectual life in the universities and elsewhere.

If the intellectual resources are there, the project of reforming moral teaching needs teachers who can refocus research and teaching in the contemporary Catholic university. There is a moral imperative to reform and reformulate moral philosophy in Catholic universities. What stands in the way?

First, the interpretation of the Second Vatican Council itself. This, as discussed earlier, was primarily concerned about the relationship between the Church and the world. The two primary documents are *Lumen gentium* (1964), on the Church herself, and *Gaudium et spes* (1965), on the relationship between the Church and the contemporary world. The two catchwords were *aggiornamento* — that is, reading the signs of the times, taking a sympathetic and pastorally open look at the world around us — and *ressourcement*, a recovery of the light of the divine revelation as graciously given us in history, particularly in the passion, death, and resurrection of Jesus Christ attested to in written form in the inspired scriptures and the patristic commentaries closest to them.

If the Council is examined in the conventional political terms of liberals versus conservatives, with the Church understood as a movement panting to "catch up" to the world, then the true message has little chance of being heard. Going back to the fonts of revelation to revitalize ourselves in them, then looking at the world as it truly is, viewing its concerns in the light of the Church's mission: that was the conciliar purpose. To do this the Council interpreted the Church as a communion, a community of faith guided by pastors and other people in conversation with Christ, not around a set of ideas as such.

Yet another obstacle to refocusing moral research and philosophical teaching is surfaced by the split in popular culture between truth and freedom. Inasmuch as individual freedom has become the most important value for Western pluralist democracies, a public judgment about the truth of a moral proposition that reduces freedom of individual choice is a threatening possibility — so threatening, in fact, that truth must be reduced from a public to a private virtue. The supreme public virtue is freedom of choice that permits, at best, a thin moral consensus that prevails only as long as it is politically possible to maintain. The Catholic intellectual tradition, on the contrary, insists that there is an intrinsic and inseparable relationship between truth and freedom, that it is beneath human dignity to live in falsehood, and that to live in religious falsehood is not only degrading but dangerous. If we worship a false god, inevitably, especially if the god is yourself, life ends in violence. Today, ironically, it is often the claim to religious truth that is regarded as the danger to peace. It is arguable that the greatest threat to freedom in both society and the university is not the Catholic faith but an insistence on living in a closed universe that claims to be the only possible world and within which nothing is accounted "reasonable" apart from that which empirical science can quantify.

A third difficulty in launching the needed reform stems from the constant tensions between the Magisterium of the bishops and those who teach in Catholic universities. This is again a question of proper autonomy — if not the personal autonomy of professors, then the autonomy of disciplines. The teaching authority of the bishops isn't based on expertise, although the bishop should be versed in theology, but his is an authority that comes from Christ. In Catholic faith, we are all related to Christ, who has authority that he has chosen to share, in part, with those ordained to govern the Church and to teach the apostolic faith in its integrity. With that authority comes a promise that the truths of faith will not be lost to the Church collectively. In that perspective, while authority based on expertise is extremely important and has to be listened to, it is not determinative for the faith community. The bishops' authority calls people to relationship, even as it is used to guarantee the truth of magisterial teaching; if the relationship of ecclesial communion is lost or weakened, the truths of faith are not life-giving.

The authority of bishops is itself, therefore, as much regulative as it is determinative. That is, the bishops point out the paths the ecclesial conversation must follow, without themselves coming to conclusions within that whole endeavor of reflection that theologians do as a matter of their own profession. The purpose of the Magisterium is to preserve the unity of the Church in revealed truth. The purpose of theologians is to explore every element of that truth and help all to see it more fully and contribute to its development. The Catholic university should be a place where that connection is desirable, a place committed to the relationship between truth and freedom. It should be a place able to explain why the human person has to be respected and what such respect demands of us as Catholics, addressing itself to a world threatened with the loss not only of truth but of many freedoms. It is, however, also a place where saints can flourish, if it is true to its identity and Catholic intellectuals are true to the fullness of their vocation.

CHAPTER 6

Education That Integrates Culture and Religion

IN THE UNITED STATES, at the mention of "religion," what people often think of first is a moral code. We're a pragmatic people; we're practical people; we're concerned about how to do things and how to act. In fact, pragmatism as a philosophy argues that theorizing follows action. Whereas classical Western wisdom stresses the thinking first and only thereupon the action that follows, Americans are very strong on action, and when it comes to defining religion, we tend to divide religions according to how they influence people's behavior. Is it a "strict" religion? Is it an "easy" religion? What does it ask you to do? What specifically does it demand that you do? Who has the right to tell you what to do?

In the society in which we live now, there aren't very many places where there is explicit reference made to what is right and what is wrong — apart from positive civil law and the libertarian manifestos that basically leave the decision to the individual. Who tells us how we are to live in a community, or how we are to live in terms of a universal moral code? Training in moral education is quite important to parents, because they can't always find help that reinforces and builds on what they as teachers themselves convey to their children; hence they are often eager to find a parochial school to assist them in this duty. Their eagerness can provide frustrations for their pastors, because the same parents who insist that their children go to a parochial school will not always bring them to Sunday worship. They see religion as moral education, and if that education has been provided at school, that's enough. Only secondarily, perhaps, is there an awareness of religion as worship of God. And yet, for people who are religious, the moral code is there because it is part of a larger vision, a vision of all that is, of the fullness of reality. Religion is a way of looking, a way of seeing, a way of thinking by which we learn what is ultimately real, what fills the universe, what is our nature, what is the ultimate purpose of our lives and of the entire created order. Religion is therefore an organizing principle for life and for knowledge. It tells us not only what we should do, but also how we should think; not only what is important, but what is true. Religion is a vision, first of all, and out of that vision comes a way of behaving.

The Christian religion is based on a faith that says that God revealed himself in history, first of all to his people, Israel, and then that historical revelation was brought to completion in the life, the death, and the resurrection from the dead of Jesus of Nazareth. Christian religion therefore demands an act of faith in a revelation that is historical and that was vouchsafed to a community. It is essentially historical and essentially communitarian. Thus understood, faith is a surrender of one's whole person, of one's self in trust to God, and the self-surrender engenders a belief that what God has revealed in history is true. We cannot grasp this completely and adequately, for "Who can know God?" Nonetheless, we come to understand it by living it, not only in what we do, but also in how we think; not only in the choices we make, but in the things we hold to be true. As we grow in righteousness we also grow in wisdom. As we become more firmly rooted in a Christian moral life, we live that life with God, the Father of Our Lord, Jesus Christ. In that sense, Christianity can be seen as a kind of praxis, always connecting orthopraxis and orthodoxy, how you act and what you think.

Christian religion may be said to include a "spirituality," but one that is historical, public, and communal. Religious spirituality is not first of all a private individual quest, which is the way we often hear spirituality referred to today. This kind of attitude toward spirituality is impossible for Christians because our relationship to the spiritual world is always mediated by our common belief; it is faith that permits us to put names on the spirit that guides us. Religion, in the Christian perspective, is not something that can be privatized, although it demands an individual response. Most especially, it's not something that reinforces individualism understood as autonomy — the word literally means "to be a law unto oneself." No one is Christian on his own terms.

How should we talk about Christian religion in the part of the intellectual life that makes use of formal education? The relationship between Christian religion and education is the subject of a conversation that has taken many forms over the ages. As we have explored, fundamentally it's a conversation between faith and reason. It's been formalized not only in pulpits, but also in institutions that would call themselves educational: monastic schools, cathedral schools, universities, spanning Christian history from the Dark Ages to the present.

There are two Latin tags that captured throughout those centuries what it meant to put faith and reason into public conversation with one another, to talk about the relationship or conversation between the Christian religion and education. The first is *fides quaerens intellectum* — that is, "faith seeking understanding." The God who gives us the gift of faith also created us with an intellect. If the faith tells us something about the way things are and about who God is — and, consequently, who we are — then faith also bids us seek to understand the world that faith has opened up. Faith seeks not only to diffuse itself but also to understand itself. For a believer, it is never enough to recite a confession of faith. Human believers are made with an intelligence that God wants us to use; and God wants us to use it to examine the faith so as to make it our own. Christian faith is supposed to be critical — not in a destructive sense, like an acid that dissolves whatever it is in contact with — but critical in its etymological sense deriving from *krisis*, the Greek word for judgment. Faith uses reason in accordance with its own norms in order to make God's self-revelation present to the intellect, to the human faculty of understanding.

Faith and reason reinforce one another in this vision of things, even when the formulations of what is presented to us by human inquiry and the formulations of what we believe by faith appear to contradict each other. The conversation goes on because there are tensions between what we believe in faith and what we come to understand from our own experience and study. Those tensions will remain until Jesus comes again in glory. But that doesn't mean that there's contradiction among the data; it means that all the data are not in, that a solution is not yet fully available. In this unresolved tension, there's a lesson for believers: not to make claims that aren't supportable. There is also a lesson for reason: not to pretend omniscience, because there are realities that reason cannot know by its own criteria. The conversation is therefore sometimes an argument. It's a conversation of long duration, however, because faith has to seek understanding. To be sure the conversation endures and is protected, educational institutions are necessary at many levels. Universities alone are not enough to guarantee the integrity of the conversation and the life it nurtures.

The second tag that characterizes Christian education pushes the conversation in ways just indicated: *credo ut intelligam*, which means, "I believe so that I can understand." Because there are things that are beyond human understanding, faith is a vision of reality larger than that given by our own experience. It's a way of understanding something that reason couldn't discover. Once revelation has helped us to see things we wouldn't see without its data, then we can begin to try to understand what has been given us by using the power of reason. I believe precisely *in order* to understand. For example, believing that I have to use my understanding to draw out the significance of declaring that Jesus is risen from the dead means that I understand differently what it means to have a human body, what it means to live and to die, what it means to be children of God in the unique and eternal Son of God. In this conversation, as mentioned above, many great universities were born:

Bologna, the first university in the Western world, followed by Paris, Oxford, and Cambridge, and Salamanca in Spain. These were the models for universities in a Christian society; they were places where Christian religion came together with formal education at a level beyond its institutionalization in home and parish.

In the nineteenth century, in Germany, another model of university was born. The modern research university is characterized by departmentalization of knowledge. This departmentalization, more than any explicit intention, caused the secularization of the university, not in the sense that the university became explicitly nonreligious, but in the sense that there was now no organizing principle beyond the specialized disciplines, no complete and unified vision of reality. Again, as was pointed out above, while the university still lay claim, by its very name, "university," to a kind of universalism of interests, what was important was to specialize so that the particular sub-branches of knowledge would advance more deeply. One of the consequences has been the kind of advance in multiple technologies that has made life in this century materially comfortable and efficient. The organizational structure of this research-oriented university was determined neither by speculative philosophy nor by a particular way of life but emerged out of the experience of conducting scientific research in the most productive ways. Knowledge became particular and historicized. We began to understand how things work not in the light of ideals from either faith or reason but from empirical observation: what are the controlling factors; who sets the agenda even for research, let alone for a curriculum?

The disjunction of the curriculum is made visible in the university itself, in the similarity of departmental structures, whether the university is a Catholic university or a state university. The disjunction of the curriculum is what tells you there isn't an operating underlying principle — whether provided by faith or by reason — notwithstanding the largely ceremonial curtsies to the value of humanist education we hear at commencement exercises or in public speeches by presidents and deans. As society becomes more and more pluralistic, such references become rarer and more timidly advanced.

Intrinsic also to this dialogue between religion and education, especially for us as Americans, is the way in which it affects our sense of freedom, which has been our primary cultural value. Where freedom is defined as freedom from any kind of external control or barriers to one's individual goals, there is no room for faith, except as an individual and private source of consolation. But if it is true that truth sets us free, then all sources of truth have to be heard and reckoned with on their own terms, even in a university. That sense of freedom opens a way into reestablishing the conversation between faith and education in the contemporary academy.

On the question of the primacy of freedom, I would argue that we have developed a cultural fault line that will continue to deepen until, in the end, the cultural and educational institutions weakened by it finally crumble and collapse. Much the same happened in Marxist societies, whose fault line was created by their willingness to sacrifice individual freedom for economic equality in the name of social justice. Social justice is not a false ideal. But a culture cannot, in the long run, advance a moral good at the expense of demanding a moral evil. One cannot sacrifice freedom, even for justice; eventually that sacrifice eroded Marxist societies from the inside. With very little external push, they simply collapsed, leaving cultural debris and very wounded people.

Do we have such a cultural fault line in our kind of liberal democracy? If there is one, it would lie in our willingness to sacrifice objective truth for subjective freedom. In that cultural perspective, any claim to universal truth, whether it be based upon a divine revelation or upon reason (a universal claim in philosophy, for example), has to be dismissed as evidence of intolerance. But this suppression of truth comes at a cost, for if there really is an absolute truth that sets us free, if there isn't antipathy between truth and freedom, then our kind of culture also is on a collision course with reality.

In this culture, what can we say about the relation between religion and educational institutions? In a Christian institution, first of all, religion provides an integrating vision, so that the institution is not just a trade school providing the tools that individual students need in order to pursue their careers. An educational institution may provide professional skills and learning in many fields, but a religiously based educational institution provides them within a context of a higher and unified vision of things that enables the student to govern his life by wisdom, and not just to learn how to make a living. Besides providing an integrating vision, religion is a regulative principle, a living guide that tells us that certain lines of thought will lead to false conclusions.

In secular educational institutions it's more complicated to talk about *fides quaerens intellectum*. One way to bring religion in is to establish special professorships or chairs. The University of Illinois at Chicago, which has had a chair of Jewish studies for several years, now has a chair in Catholic studies. That initiative has been well received because the university governance, the dean especially, was eager to have such a chair, not because they were searching for an integrating vision, but because they retain the idea of the university as a place to listen to all voices. Where ideological pluralism is viewed as a positive attribute for the university, even a faith community might have a voice there. Through using an instrument that the university understands, an endowed and restricted chair, one gets a voice, and that permits a conversation between religion and education to take place.

A second way into a secular university is through campus ministry or, more recently, through institutes or centers of Catholic thought established by Catholic scholars. Campus ministry provides the context for the Church leaders not only to bring the solace of religion to individual students but also to bear witness to truth, and even to teach. In the early history of Newman clubs on secular campuses, the intellectual mission was central, though beginning in the 1960s it was neglected. More recently, Catholic scholars have founded institutes of Catholic thought to present the Catholic intellectual life as lived in a faith tradition while engaging the culture of the secular university. Inspired by the Lumen Christi Institute for Catholic Thought — established by Catholic scholars in 1997 — Robert Wilken founded the St. Anselm Institute at the University of Virginia. Of the new possibilities thus opened he writes:

I sensed the unique role such an institute could play in the university when I was invited to give a lecture at the Lumen Christi Institute at the University of Chicago. The topic was Catholicism and Western culture, and the lecture was held in a classroom in Swift Hall on the main quadrangle of the university. When I was a student in the divinity school there, I often had classes in that room, and it was a new experience to see it filled with students and faculty who had come to hear a lecture sponsored by a Catholic institute.

In that setting, I sensed a freedom about what could be said. It was possible to deal with the topic in an explicitly Catholic way and from a Catholic perspective. Yet it was still a university lecture, and the audience certainly expected it to be as scholarly as other lectures given in that same room under different auspices.... A Catholic institute is no less a forum for debate and argument than is the rest of the university. Catholic tradition is a living thing to be contested as well as upheld, not a genteel legacy to be perfumed and powdered.[1]

Third, even a secular university must come to terms with the fact that the history of various disciplines is bound up with the faith. In the development of philosophy, psychology, and anthropology, the humanities as well as much of science, one finds a history that brings a body of knowledge into conversation, sometimes a very difficult conversation, with Christian faith. One finds questions that at least some of the scientists and scholars want to pursue by bringing into the discussion people of faith who also understand their discipline. Some of that discussion is made possible by reason of the history of universities as well as the history of the various fields of study. There are also incidental ways in which the university will call upon the faith community to enter into a conversation that the university couldn't have on its own. It will do this more readily if the religious

1. Robert Louis Wilken, "Catholic Scholars, Secular Schools," *First Things* 179 (January 2008): 40–43.

community has made evident that, because of faith, believers have a deep respect for reason — and respect, therefore, for the university as a place where truth is sought and passed on.

If we understand the Christian religion in the way that I describe it, then any university is an important place for any of us; and if the university understands that the community of faith has deep respect for the community of learning, a conversation becomes possible. When you enter into the conversation, you bring a critique, you raise the question about an integrating principle; and many academics are quite concerned about that question as they watch their disciplines unravel into methodologies more and more disparate and the possibility of genuine conversation about first-order questions slip from their grasp.

Christian faith gives a confidence in the ability of the human intellect to discover truth. That might seem obvious, but that ability is denied in many parts of the academic world today. A service to truth that the faith brings consists in teaching us that we have been made intelligent beings by a God who expects us to use our reason. Therefore, we should have confidence that we can discover truth. The conviction that one cannot know anything as true, that all our judgments are opinion, is destructive of human life. It leads first to cynicism and then to nihilism. The kind of philosophizing popularized by Nietzsche in one generation contributed to the rise of Nazism in the next. St. John Paul II often said that we should have confidence and not be afraid, because we are able to discover and know the truth. We can have confidence, therefore, in our ability to face up to history and change it. This is the pope speaking as a missionary. The same pope wrote that we should have confidence in our ability to live intimately with God and with one another. That's the pope speaking as a mystic. Because God has graciously revealed who he is in Jesus, Son of God and Son of Mary, we shouldn't be afraid of intimacy with one another. Don't be afraid that your reason is not up to the task of knowing all things, as Aristotle said; and also don't be afraid that your heart may not be able to embrace all those whom God loves — that is to say, everyone. The universal terms "everything," "everyone," make sense within the vision given us by the Christian faith.

In our progressively more globalized society, capital, persons, ideas move around the world with greater and greater ease. Contacts, of course, are not relationships, but if we allow contacts to develop into ever more universal relationships, then the relationships generated by shared faith are going to become more important than the relationships that are now based upon citizenship. What will be the carrier of culture in the millennium ahead? Not nation-states, as we have known them for the past five hundred years. The conversation creating culture will be one that is carried on by the great faiths. Along with the great faiths, however, the great universities have become more and more self-conscious about their role as carriers of culture.

The problematic set out by the *status quaestionis*, as résuméd here, clarifies a great and persistent challenge. Must formal education, at all levels, insistently continue along a course of secularization and alienation? The answer is no, if the community of believers is able to contribute to a conversation between faith and reason that will rescue formal education from its present deficiencies. For those who love both faith and reason, it is painful to watch the unnecessary self-destruction of our greatest cultural and educational institutions because the faith community can't find a way to offer its own critique more convincingly. This failure has prevented the Church from implementing the dialogical vision of the Second Vatican Council, with its intended universal impact.

In all conversations creating culture, the Church should be able to be an honest observer and a participant, bringing to the table our concern for a common language giving voice to our concern that languages and other intellectual divisions will become so specialized, so disparate, that we will lose the ability to talk across differences of academic disciplines, national differences, racial differences, religious differences. Unfortunately, our Catholic "common" language still sounds sectarian in the public conversation today. The Catholic Church, when it enters into conversation with the larger society, tries not to use specifically ecclesiastical language. It tries, instead, to use a language based upon what has been called natural law; we've been no more successful, however, than was St. Paul when he first used this approach two thousand years ago. Even though attempts to find a language that can be heard by "all people of good will" have not yet succeeded, this remains a challenge at the center of the concerns of anyone who brings together personally the life of the fully developed human mind and heart and belief in the God who reveals himself as the creator and redeemer of the entire human race. Returning, finally, to the Second Vatican Council as the contemporary context for the conversation between faith and reason should help in finding a response to this challenge.

CHAPTER 7

Integrating the Second Vatican Council

WORDS BOTH REPORT and create realities. Taking the Second Vatican Council at its word, it was called to change the world by changing the Church so that she could talk to everyone. The pastoral and intellectual challenge is to be effectively engaged in shaping the world without being simply co-opted or caught up in the perspective of the age itself. Believers cannot be a closed cell of votaries talking only to themselves, but neither are they to be chaplains to the status quo. The Church's pastoral and intellectual challenge, along with offering personal direction to believers, is to have a public life that is true to the Lord, meeting the world's concerns as Christ himself would meet them. The Church has authority from Christ to speak in his name. When the Church becomes just one more pressure group, she loses her true identity.

One path to loss of ecclesial identity is for the Church to abandon her intellectual mission and seek legitimacy from society by allowing herself to be absorbed into service. This is something the world will praise: we have good schools, we go a long way to help the poor, we have admirable works of charity and healing. But if the Church's mission is absorbed into providing services, there's no call to conversion. What is usually not understood is the call to leave everything, even the good things, so as to follow Christ. The Church's ongoing commitment to the conversation between faith and reason helps save the Church from this temptation and puts her mission in perspective.

Conversion to Christ is conversion to newness of life with him who is the same yesterday, today, and forever. Believers are not absorbed by the primary realities of their life but are brought into divine continuity. This continuity is what Pope Benedict XVI wanted to emphasize in presenting the methodology of the Council itself as an example of the hermeneutic of reform. Pope Benedict, during a talk to the Roman Curia in 2005, spoke of development of doctrine; but the developments, the changes, are in continuity with historical revelation, even as changing practices in life and worship are in continuity with the constant teaching of the Church herself. Without her self-understanding based upon reforms rather than rupture, the Church has nothing original to offer to the conversation between faith and reason.[1] Moreover, if the connections between

1. Benedict XVI, "Address to the Roman Curia Offering them his Chris-

belief and practice are not clear, there will inevitably be discontinuity in belief and chaos in practice.

Pope Benedict spoke of a common lens of interpretation or "hermeneutic" applied to the Council, which he termed a hermeneutic of rupture. This distorting lens sees a pre-conciliar Church and a post-conciliar Church with little or no historical continuity between them, as if the Church began anew in the Council. The hermeneutic of rupture interprets the Council as an event animated by a certain spirit. In this view, the conciliar texts themselves are inadequate expressions of the Council, and we should look instead to what was happening in the Church and accept the spirit of the event as normative and as interpretative for pastoral practice.

Of course, the Council was an event; it was the major religious event of the twentieth century and was enlivened by many spirits. The challenge is to fit these into an organic development, a relationship with revelation, and with the tradition that connects us to it, and with the practice that bears witness to faith in what God has revealed. In other words, every Catholic is born two thousand years old and, more than that, every Catholic is born with the memories that shaped Christ himself, memories extending back to the Hebrew prophets, to Moses, to Abraham, Isaac, and Jacob. Finally, the con-

mas Greetings," *The Holy See*, http://w2.vatican.va/content/benedict-xvi/en/speeches/2005/december/documents/hf_ben_xvi_spe_20051222_roman-curia.html.

ciliar texts are normative within the Church's constant interpretation of them. The texts are not simply parliamentary documents. Once the Council is over, the texts are given to the Church's pastors so they can apply them in the Church's life and mission. This is a call to real change. A change, however, was already evident in the style of the texts themselves, and this fact is responsible for some of the force in the appeal to the spirit of the Council.

Most conciliar texts in the twenty ecumenical councils before the Second Vatican Council were terse and canonical in their expression. In the Second Vatican Council, much of the pastoral work of exhorting and persuading was put into the texts themselves. It was a pastoral council and, since not every pastoral exhortation is normative, some documents were composed in a looser rhetorical style that was novel. When there is a change of style in Council documents, expectations can emerge about a change in substance.

When there is a change in expository manner, there is at least the possibility of raising questions about the substance being expounded. For the Second Vatican Council there is an opening in the documents themselves for the kind of multiple competing interpretations, some of them contrary to the wishes of the Council itself, that have burdened the Church's pastoral and intellectual life in the last fifty years. A description of this hermeneutic of rupture is deftly given by Fr. John O'Malley, SJ, the Jesuit historian who wrote an engaging and convincing book about what happened at the Council.[2] He skillfully gave credence to both sides in interpreting the Council, but he espoused the kind of break that Pope Benedict XVI would not think helpful, because it would be closer to the hermeneutic of rupture than it is to the hermeneutic of reform. How did Fr. O'Malley explain these two approaches? "At stake, almost, are two different versions of Catholicism: from commands to invitations, from laws to ideals, from definition to mystery, from threats to persuasion, from coercion to conscience, from monologue to dialogue, from ruling to serving, from withdrawn to integrated, from vertical to horizontal, from exclusion to inclusion, from hostility to friendship, from rivalry to partnership, from suspicion to trust, from static to ongoing, from passive acceptance to active engagement, from fault-finding to appreciation, from restrictive to principled, from behavior modification to inner-appropriation."[3] The list is a caricature by oversimplification, and Fr. O'Malley knows he is making a point. It's very effective, however, because there's truth to it. The Council signaled a shift in pastoral attitude and

2. John W. O'Malley, SJ, *What Happened at Vatican II?* (Cambridge, Mass.: Harvard University Press, 2010), 307.
3. Ibid.

approach to the world. The Council's purpose, though, was not to undo the past and to leave open questions that the Church had previously settled in the course of her history of doctrinal development.

Pope Benedict asked in his 2005 talk to the Roman Curia, "Why has the implementation of the Council in large parts of the Church thus far been so difficult? The problems in its implementation arose from the fact that two contrary hermeneutics came face-to-face and quarreled with each other. One caused confusion, the other silently but more and more visibly bore and is bearing fruit." The pope believes that, but he says it almost wistfully, for we have lost decades in distraction in internal squabbles.

The Council, as Pope Benedict said, is not a constituent assembly, because the essential constitution of the Church has come from the Lord himself. Bishops are not originators of revelation; they are stewards of the Lord's gifts. Where the idea is paramount that bishops are parliamentarians, a political interpretation of the Council is given and the pastoral life of the Church risks becoming dominated by various pressure groups, each wanting to get enough bishops on its side. If bishops and other pastors don't cooperate, they must be blind or stupid. Pastoral governance becomes difficult because the bishops' proper authority is undercut. The authority that any bishop has comes from Christ, and the authority to teach through a Council is also from Christ. The pope himself is steward of the Lord's gifts; he is not master of the Church, as Benedict has said more than once. Therefore we have to move beyond and around a false hermeneutic, often expounded in political terms, and explore the hermeneutic of reform.

Benedict reviewed the history of the relationship between the Church and the world, particularly in the modern era. When the political interpretation of the Council as a debate between conservative and liberal factions was resisted and it was clear that the Council's purpose was also to challenge modernity from within modernity itself, the pastoral tensions began in earnest. Basically, the hermeneutic of reform, as the pope explained it, paints a continuity of principle in changing circumstances. A discontinuity of situation — for example, the vast earthquake of the French Revolution — calls for a development in the Church's understanding of the apostolic faith. But the developments in understanding the faith anew are based upon principles, valid in all circumstances. From the viewpoint of the papacy, the French Revolution defined modernity, and the Revolution's antagonisms were as much against the Church as against the king. Thousands of priests and nuns were murdered, convents were destroyed, and inevitably the Church started off very badly in its dialogue with the modern world, as shaped by the French Revolution and its European aftershocks. Today, modernity itself has become more self-critical. The hubris of the French Revolution quickly dissolved in bloodshed that engulfed all of Europe, and many, thus chastened, began to establish a better framework for understanding history than the Revolution itself gave. This dialogue between the continuity of the principles — *ressourcement* — and the discontinuity of a particular historical situation — *aggiornamento* — establishes the hermeneutic of reform. It enters into the heart of the dialogue between faith and reason, our generation's contribution to the conversation at the heart of the Church and in the soul of the believer.

A hermeneutic of reform suggests caution before changing religious practices. Whether out of naiveté or out of generosity of spirit, bishops around the world often destroyed common customs, religious cultural markers, and replaced them with individual choice. A case in point would be Friday abstinence from meat. It was a Catholic community marker, as well as a religious act of penitence. A powerfully integrative practice of common penance helped keep everybody in the same community. When the discipline was dropped in the United States, what did the bishops here say? They explained continuity remained in the new regulation: we should all do penance on Friday; but it's now up to the individual to determine what that act of penance will be.

We have a common value, if you like, but we don't have common behavior. It's hard to keep a common value when the community no longer shares in common behavior.[4]

It's also hard to keep continuity in doctrinal meaning when its expression is changed. It can be done, the faith can be expressed in diverse ways; but the practical abandonment of a common liturgical and doctrinal language has put strain on our unity in the faith. Because the assumption for reform seemed to be that a practice or a belief is more personal when freely chosen, the governing and teaching authority of the bishops was inadvertently weakened, for the bishops' role is to pass on what they have received and to encourage its acceptance from generation to generation until Christ returns in glory to judge the living and the dead.

A secular crisis developed when the Council changed the Church's relation to the world for the sake of evangelizing. Evangelizing the world means changing the world, but only after listening to a world created and loved by God yet also steeped in sin. The listening became "catching up," and the renewal, too often, became self-secularization. That was especially true in religious

4. An observation of the anthropologist Robert Redfield may be apposite here: "[Men] cease to believe because they cease to understand, and they cease to understand because they cease to do the things that express the understandings"; Redfield, *The Folk Culture of the Yucatan* (Chicago: University of Chicago Press, 1941), 363.

communities of apostolic life. A way of life that was distinctive and confident enough to create a mission-focused identity — both personal and social — all but disintegrated.

The bishops tried to put toothpaste back in the tube when they encouraged Friday abstinence in order to sacrifice for world peace.[5] The admonition had no effect at all. It was yet another personal choice, not an activity to be done out of obedience to the Church. The collapse of common witness mandated by episcopal authority left many with the idea that the Church can't command anything in their life. After all, the sin of eating meat on Friday was a sin of disobedience. In the end, it doesn't matter much what the religious custom is, but it makes all the difference if the action is done out of obedience or out of a purely personal choice. If you choose it individually, you're an autonomous actor making your own path in your own way. If you do it out of obedience, you're a disciple and united to disciples in all the ages. Such change in pastoral practice created many of the difficulties in properly understanding the purpose of the Council.

The hermeneutic of rupture undermined the Church's

5. "As a tangible sign of our need and desire to do penance we, for the cause of peace, commit ourselves to fast and abstinence on each Friday of the year"; *The Challenge of Peace: God's Promise and Our Response; A Pastoral Letter on War and Peace*, National Conference of Catholic Bishops (U.S.A), May 3, 1983, para. 298.

pastoral authority as well. Pastors don't just advise spiritually; they govern, with help from many friends and counselors, but nonetheless the pastor is to govern. The Reformation was fought on how the Church is to be governed. In the lands that accepted the teaching of Luther, for whom the Church was regarded as a purely internal spiritual reality, the external governance of the Church was given over to the prince-protector. That sense of the Church as a purely spiritual association remains part of our American consciousness, because we are still culturally a Protestant nation.

If the Church has no claim to her own law because she is merely an internal spiritual community, a kind of a club formed by those who are touched by the Holy Spirit and therefore brought to salvation one by one, gathering in ways that are adventitious to the Gospel itself, then the form of governing the Church is up to every community in every age to decide anew. An assembly can vote a regulation up or vote it down, and, absent a sacrament of Holy Orders as a reality check for our common life, it can do the same for a doctrine. Governance has therefore become problematic in recent years. Pastoral government's task now was to present something that is good with the hope that its very goodness would be attractive and convince everyone of its truth. But people can see a good presented to them, not understand it as good, and prefer to go their own way. If the ministry of the Church depends upon achieving contemporary consensus, the mission of the Church loses its impetus.

A crisis in catechesis paralleled the crisis of ecclesiastical government. After the Council, catechesis was examined and found to be too filled with anti-Protestant apologetics overly concerned to show that the Reformation was wrong. Catechesis was renewed by going back to the sources of revelation. The beauty of the truth was to be persuasive on its own; it had only to be presented, without apologetics. That was attempted and, in fact, it was often well done. The problem remains that to tell people what we do believe, we also have to tell them what we don't believe. Without some negative guidelines for discerning doctrinal truth, people will feel free to make up new Christs. The Church must be able to say, "That is wrong," as well as saying, "This is right," and must do so in a lucid, less defensive way. Catholic bishops have reintroduced apologetics into catechesis so that instructors can start with what is true and also point out what is false. To implement the Council more effectively, we should recognize mistakes in governing and teaching in the last half-century and continue to correct them.

We should also, secondly, understand the authentic doctrinal development in the Council's teaching. On this issue Catholics separate themselves from Msgr. Lefebvre and his followers, who insist that the formulation of a truth or the practice of the liturgy must be exactly what they were when they themselves were first led to believe, ignoring the history of that formulation and the development of doctrine over the ages.

We find genuine development, for example, in the Second Vatican Council's teaching about the sacrament of holy orders. The Council fathers were concerned to show how the nature of the priesthood is to refocus and incarnate in a particular ordained priest's life Christ's own relationship to the Church. This shift complemented Aquinas's insistence that the priest is primarily identified by reference to the Eucharistic body of Christ in his power to consecrate; it emphasized instead the priest's authority to govern the body of Christ that is the Church. The first priestly virtue is pastoral charity.

In addition to doctrinal developments, there was the anthropological turn to be found in the Vatican II documents *Dignitatis humanae* (1965) and *Gaudium et spes* that was to be elaborated by later popes and theologians. In the teaching of John Paul II, man is the way of the Church, but Christ tells us who man is in the various cultures that are the expression of a group's nonbiological inheritance. Pope John Paul II showed us how to maintain the apostolic teaching and still reformulate it in a way that brings something forward that previously hadn't been seen. His whole magisterium was an expression of the Church's teaching in the light of the Council.

When John Paul II wanted to demonstrate the Council in action, he pointed to Mother Teresa of Calcutta. She was the Good Samaritan for our age, and the spirituality of the Council was that of the Good Samaritan, as Pope Paul VI said at the closing of the Council.[6] Pope Francis uses the image of Church as field hospital, binding up the wounds of the world.[7] When John Paul marked his twenty-fifth anniversary as Bishop of Rome, he wanted to celebrate the occasion while beatifying Mother Teresa, because, he said, she expressed the meaning of the Council and therefore the meaning of his papacy. The cardinals told him that he had to have two celebrations: Mother Teresa's beatification one month and his anniversary celebration later. The pope accepted that advice, but there was no separation in his own mind between his own papacy and her ministry, his teaching and her witness to Christ as a Good Samaritan attending to the poor of our time.

To deepen in our day the conversation between faith and reason, the Church needs not only to examine the

6. Paul VI, "Address During the Last General Meeting of the Second Vatican Council," *The Holy See*, http://w2.vatican.va/content/paul-vi/en/speeches/1965/documents/hf_p-vi_spe_19651207_epilogo-concilio.html.

7. Antonio Spadero, "A Big Heart Open to God: The Exclusive Interview with Pope Francis," *America*, September 30, 2013, http://americamagazine.org/pope-interview.

blunders in pastoral practice after the Council and try to correct them, and not only examine as well the authentic development that the Second Vatican Council brought about in theological understanding of the mysteries of faith; the Church needs also to ask how, in the light of the hermeneutic of reform, her pastors are to address the questions put to them by believers.

Such questions are of two sorts. The first kind concerns the continuing validity of the tradition that unites us to Christ. Many of the Church's teachings have been regarded with skepticism by the modern age and, not coincidentally, questioned by different schools and theologians within the Church. Very often people ask questions like these: Why does the Catholic Church have so many rules? I'm divorced, why can't I go to Holy Communion? Why is the Church opposed to science — for example, stem cell research and artificial contraception? Why isn't the Catholic Church more biblically based? Why are women unequal in the Church, since they can't be ordained priests? Why does the Church make religion and spirituality so complicated? Can't I just believe in God and live a good life? Why should I confess my sins to a priest? These are all important questions. Some emerge from a Protestant sensibility, others from a secularist worldview, still others suggest injury inflicted by poor pastoral practice on the part of a priest. Those are the kinds of questions all priests have to answer, and many lay Catholics have to confront them, too.

There is no shortage of books, pamphlets, and magazines that respond to these questions in order to clarify the faith for believers and make them active participants in the faith-reason dialogue. They provide a form of apologetics that helps the Church internally to rethink the questions of the age in such a way as to assure the faithful. Those questions are part of pastoral life now because of the hermeneutic of rupture, no doubt, but also because the hermeneutic of reform itself invites us to distinguish between the continuity of principle and the discontinuity of situation. Questions arise from dilemmas that reflect the concrete difficulties believers experience in living their faith. Good pastoral practice seeks to apply the relevant principle to the situation and interpret it in fidelity to the demands of discipleship.

There is a second set of questions that gets to the heart of the hermeneutic of reform, focusing on the mission of the Church herself. One such question is: What is the connection between Jesus and the Church? This connection was broken by the leaders of the Reformation in the West, and it's been questioned even within the Catholic Church over the centuries. Or again, what is the connection between the Church and the Kingdom of God in the teaching of Jesus? When I studied ecclesiology, as the Council was beginning, the Gospel parables of the kingdom were simply assumed to be speaking of the Church. Today the relationship would be explained with attention to distinctions between immanent and eschatological aspects of the Church and of God's Lordship. Nevertheless, the pastoral challenge is to help people understand that they cannot accept Jesus as a personal savior without accepting the Church, which is his body. Jesus doesn't come alone, and we don't go back to him alone. The Church mediates our relationship to Jesus.

A third question is: how does faith make a difference in dealing with the difficulties of life: suffering, death, sin — the evils that the Lord spoke about in the Gospel and that are with us today? How does faith make a difference in dealing with the tough stuff of life? The problem of evil is part of the experience of the human race, and the persistence of evil is a primary objection to the teaching that God is good and all-powerful. The heart of the response to evil that our faith gives us is Christ crucified. God saves us through suffering. But that remains abstract and pastorally inadequate unless one can in fact join those who suffer so as to understand from within the experience of evil.

Another question arises from uncertainty about how the sacraments put us in touch with God. The Eucharist is still a lodestone for Catholics, but when one considers marriage, penance, and holy orders, the felt contact with God is no longer so evident. To understand continuity of principle with discontinuity of situation, pastors must confront individualism in religion, which defines the cultural situation here. Many believers in the post-Enlightenment West preserve traces of that Pelagian instinct by which a man approaches God by, so to speak, mounting a ladder of his own devising; it is difficult for such persons to experience the sacraments as occasions of divine rather than human initiative, as channels of grace instituted by God rather than here-and-now ceremonies of their own contrivance.

A fifth question deals with the importance accorded sexual morality and marriage in Catholic faith. Why are we now constantly talking about it? How is it that marriage has broken down, that divorce is prevalent, that so many children are born out of wedlock? From this lived situation, how do we point to the truth of the principle?

A final question is: What does it mean to live in this world as a citizen, as a worker, as a parent, as a believer on the path to personal holiness? The vocation to holiness is universal; we are all called to be saints. But there is a pronounced shift in the Council's emphasis on holiness in the world and not only in flight from the world.

Five decades after the Council, the entire Church but especially her pastors need to attend to the multiform and sometimes contradictory developments in seeking a communal Catholic way of life. Lay people especially are calling the attention of their pastors to the centrality of the Eucharist, including Eucharistic adoration, in creating a Catholic sense of community. In the aftermath of the Council, an unfortunate rivalry emerged between liturgy and devotion, sometimes attended by an almost sectarian factionalism. Faithful Catholics know that these two forms of worship belong together. While not every initiative in the Church is supposed to come from the pastors, the preservation of unity is their responsibility, and their oversight of ministry and devotion must always attend to unity. The faith is practiced together.

The purpose of good pastoring is to keep people united around Jesus Christ. Then the Church can be a leaven in the world, which was the principal reason for calling the Second Vatican Council. The pastoral question that pastors have to ask themselves when deciding their own activity or discussing the action of others is: Will this action unite or will it divide in the long run? When changing customs and practices, pastors have to show the relationship to what is presently done and taught, so that a rupture does not occur in the life of the Church and in the minds and hearts of believers. This is a necessary condition if the centuries-old conversation that unites us to Christ is to be effective today and tomorrow.

Benedict XVI explained what the Church is to be in light of the Second Vatican Council's contribution to her self-understanding today: "A missionary Church known for proclaiming her message to all peoples and therefore necessarily working for the freedom of the faith."[8]

8. Benedict XVI, "Address to the Roman Curia."

CHAPTER 8

Recent Popes and the Renewal of Catholic Intellectual Life

IF THE SECOND VATICAN COUNCIL's contribution to the dialogue between faith and reason in our day has to be understood as a word of continuity in principle, with recognition of discontinuity in situations, then it is equally important to recognize how the situation has been redefined by the Magisterium and ministry of Pope St. John Paul II. Seldom has a papacy been so grounded in guiding the conversation between faith and reason and in showing how, in the life of the pope himself, intellectual and spiritual lives are intertwined.

In the American scheme of things, the pope is often regarded as primarily an authority figure, a bit of a taskmaster. Religion is something that tells people what to do and is often interpreted as legalistic rather than visionary. Stories about popes often portray them as autocrats striving to restrain the individual believer struggling to break free of religious authority. In the soft secularism that characterizes our culture now, religious authority is a threat to human freedom — as is God himself, for if God is powerful, then he is a threat to human freedom, our competitor in governing the world. For that kind of secularism, the social goal is to contain God. But if such is our only approach to the papacy, it not only keeps us perpetually adolescent in matters religious, forever in revolt against authority, it also fails in understanding the role of the popes as bearers of a vision that gives us insight into the ways of God.

The vision of the late Pope St. John Paul II will influence the Catholic imagination for generations to come. He reworked the tradition in ways that wouldn't have been possible without his particular experience and without his intellectual background. In the grand scheme of the Church's constant search for ways of imaging God, who finally escapes our way of understanding, the Church has in John Paul's life and thought both continuity and change.

There are two parts to this examination. First, a few reflections on the Enlightenment's splitting of concept and image. This division has dominated intellectual life for several centuries, and Pope John Paul II was concerned to resolve it. This split must be overcome, I would argue, in order to renew culture in ways adequate to the capacities of the human person. We needn't go into a scientific exploration of what is a concept and what is an image. One is abstract, one is more concrete, and there are many ways of relating them. But if they are totally separated, as is the case in several strands of Enlightenment philosophy, then poetry becomes merely subjectivistic, mere self-expression, rather than a way of reaching and describing objective reality in respects superior to purely conceptual expression. Why did this pope continue to write poetry? He wrote poems expressing his reflections on the conclave in the Sistine Chapel that elected him pope and poems on the future conclave in the light of the history of salvation, poems on God's creation, man's fall, and Christ's redemptive death, poems on resurrection and coming again in glory. Not everybody was aware of this, as he didn't publish under his name as priest and bishop, but he was a practicing poet whose poetry reflected his faith and his ministry.

What does that tell us about John Paul's understanding of how God and man continue to move forward in history, and how the life of the mind contributes to our life with God? It speaks to the pope's conviction that, epistemologically at least, if we're going to overcome division between God and man, if we're going to understand either faith or intellect more fully, then we have to engage all our capacities for knowing. If we keep concept and image as distinct as Enlightenment thought gives them to us, we can't see the links in the notion of being itself. God therefore becomes either totally unknown, or else demoted to the level of just another being and, moreover, a being that is different in being "Supreme." In analyzing the pope's own words and the images evoked by them in his plays and poetry, we discover something of the inner culture of John Paul II. Why would Karol Wojtyła use images of God in the way he did? What does that tell us about his own interior dialogue, his own interior life and the conversation that shaped him as a thinker and as a believer?

Since the time of the Enlightenment, it has been widely presumed that thoughtful people had two choices before them: either to swear allegiance to religious faith and so renounce investment in the human project, or else to swear allegiance to reason and so renounce commitment to religious faith.

A well-known media commentator in America, reacting to Pope John Paul's 1998 encyclical *Fides et ratio*, wrote in a syndicated column, "Why is this pope writing a letter on faith and reason? Everybody knows that faith is feeling and reason is logic and there is no connection between them at all." This is an expression, in very popular form, of Western intellectual development since the Enlightenment, and even of a certain strain of religiosity, accepted as fact even by many who identify themselves as believers.

One can trace this development back before the Enlightenment, to the work of the Jesuit theologian Francisco Suarez (1548–1617) or even to Duns Scotus (1266–1308) who, arguing against Aquinas, insisted on the univocity of being. But for Scotus, there is one and only one concept for each word — even for being itself — that is therefore an abstract notion divorced from all particulars. Aquinas could say that God "is," but he "is" in a way that is radically different from any way that we "are" and therefore is not in competition with us as beings. The Thomistic concept of being is not univocal but analogical. We understand God in concepts that include images and convey various levels of content. Man is not in ontological competition with God. God is the precondition of our freedom, as he is of our existence. The universe of words, therefore, needs analogous predication, because beings truly are different. If, however, being is univocal in its meaning, God becomes a Supreme Being among the existents, and therefore a potential competitor. One can in fact portray later intellectual history as an attempt by philosophers and theologians to read into the human mind the characteristics that medieval theologians attributed to the mind of God. Thus the myth of progress is a parable in which man takes back God's power over nature by means of his own ingenuity — science, technology, political coercion — thus establishing his freedom, understood as autonomy: personal and political independence from God.

But it wasn't always the case that men viewed being

as radically splintered in this way. Consider the angels: in their own right they are cosmologically interesting, inasmuch as they fill in the great chain of being extending from infinite spiritual reality (God) through a finite spiritual reality (the angels) into finite embodied spiritual beings (ourselves) and then into finite material beings that have no spirit. And apart from their cosmological interest, angels are beings through whose agency God protects us, cares for us, enables us to be free, sustains us in existence. They are evidence that God is not out to get us.

Karol Wojtyła was obviously a man of faith, and he was trained philosophically. He was professor of ethics at Lublin University in Poland. He matured intellectually in an environment of struggle with a Marxist regime for which all ideation was rigorously subordinated to the goal of producing the new socialist state. Although he had theological training, it's fair to say that John Paul II seemed to take his intellectual direction more from philosophy, and specifically philosophical anthropology, than from theology. But his was a philosophy practiced always by a believer. He was therefore well equipped to synthesize the polarities of religious faith and humanistic commitment and to reexamine the relationship between concepts and images. He was a philosopher — a man of concepts; and a poet — a man of images. More to the point, he was able to let each inform the other.

The search for a synthesis, the hope for a reconciliation of human and divine causality and concerns, is set forth programmatically in an encyclical from the early years of his pontificate, *Dives in misericordia*, his letter on God the Father. This letter talks about God as conceptualized and imaged in his mercy. The pope wrote, "In Jesus Christ, every path to man, as it has been assigned once and for all to the Church in the changing context of the times, is simultaneously an approach to the Father and to His love. The Second Vatican Council has confirmed this truth for our time. The more the Church's mission is centered upon man — the more it is, so to speak, anthropocentric — the more it must be confirmed and actualized theocentrically, that is to say, to be directed through Jesus Christ to God, the Merciful Father. While the various currents of human thought both in the past and in the present have tended and still tend to separate theocentrism and anthropocentrism, and even to set them into opposition to each other, the Church, following Christ, seeks to link them up in human history in a deep and organic way. And this is also one of the basic principles — perhaps the most important one — of the teaching of the last Council."[1]

The particular linkage of the human and the divine in the pope's thinking was already evident in the encyc-

1. John Paul II, *Dives in misericordia* (Rome: Typis Polyglottis Vaticanis, 1980), 1.

lical that he wrote shortly after he was elected to the Chair of St. Peter. In *Redemptor hominis* (*The Redeemer of Mankind*), John Paul says, "Man cannot live without love. He remains a being that is incomprehensible for himself, his life is senseless if love is not revealed to him, if he does not encounter love, if he does not experience it, and then make it his own, if he does not participate intimately in it. This is why Christ the Redeemer 'fully reveals man to himself.' . . . This is the human dimension of the mystery of the Redemption. In this dimension, man finds again the greatness, dignity, and value that belong to his humanity. . . . In reality, the name for that deep amazement at man's worth and dignity is the Gospel, that is to say: the Good News. It is also called Christianity and this amazement determines the Church's mission in the world. . . . This amazement, which is also a conviction and a certitude — at its deepest root it is the certainty of faith, but in a hidden and mysterious way it vivifies every aspect of authentic humanism — is closely connected with Christ. It also fixes Christ's place, his particular right of citizenship — in the history of the human race."[2]

What emerges therefore with great consistency in the writings and talks of John Paul II is a God who is preoccupied with humanity, who takes his creation to

2. John Paul II, *Redemptor hominis* (Rome: Typis Polyglottis Vaticanis, 1979), 10.

heart, who desires that it be healed and that it flourish, who is a source of amazement and of wonder. Consistently, he spoke of "God's plan" or "God's will" directed to humanity. In another encyclical letter, *Ut unum sint*, on Christian ecumenism, he wrote, "The unity of all divided humanity is the will of God."[3]

In John Paul II's writing on the permanent validity of the Church's missionary mandate — which is to unite every man in Christ — he appeals to God's plan for humanity as the foundation for all his reflections. In his encyclical *Redemptoris missio* (1990), God, who is preoccupied with all of humanity, can be called a humanist God. This "picture" of God does not emerge in the magisterial writings of John Paul II through the use of special images, like the biblical images. Nor does the humanist God emerge in any form of mystical analogy as such. Although we're discussing an author who has written on St. John of the Cross, the pope didn't use the tie between intimate lovers to image the relationship between God and man. In fact, John Paul II presents the humanist God through an insistent narrative of God's action on behalf of the human race. Mankind's destiny as healed, transformed, unified, and called to happiness in this life and the next is the source of John Paul's vocabulary. In some sense, the pope followed the

3. John Paul II, *Ut unum sint* (Rome: Typis Polyglottis Vaticanis, 1995), note 6.

program of his phenomenological work in *The Acting Person* (*Person and Act*), by identifying God's "operative" values through and in his action, especially in sending Jesus Christ to be our savior. I shall return to *The Acting Person* in order to link the imagery of his plays and early poetry with his philosophical work.

If God is a humanist, the other side of the equation is that humanists should be godly. The humanist God and the godly humanist, the God who is intimately preoccupied with the human race, and human beings who are concerned about their own identity and future, represent the polarities of theocentrism and anthropocentrism that John Paul II sought to integrate in God's action and in ours. Who is the godly humanist in the writings of John Paul II? Authentic human concern, according to him, will inevitably lead one back to the foundations of human dignity in divine transcendence. This is a spirituality of humanism that opens one up self-consciously to a God who reveals to us who we ourselves truly are — through his generosity, his love, his action on our behalf. In a reversal of Feuerbach, one can state that authentic anthropology must necessarily be theology.

The godly humanist is possessed of an interior culture or spirituality that is shaped by a generosity that is the deepest image, the deepest sign of God's image and likeness in us. If we live generously, our actions will disclose to us who we are as created in God's image and likeness if they're done self-consciously, if they're done reflectively, if we know who we are in acting generously. We will, in our very experience of ourselves in act, close the gap between supernatural faith and natural humanism as one becomes through his actions the image of a generous God. That is why the pope began the encyclical *Fides et ratio* with the old Greek dictum, "Know thyself."

A life shaped by generous action, whether by divine generosity or human generosity, can be described or traced by human words. Precisely as human beings, who first are named by God, who name the created world, like Adam giving the beasts their names, we name things we did not make and then, through human words, create other worlds in poetry and fiction and in great works of discovery. It is necessary, therefore, to search for images of God not only in created nature and in the generosity of our own actions, imitating a God who creates us out of nothing because he loves us, but also in our wordsmithing, in our own vocabulary. Karol Wojtyła originally planned to devote his life to the study of Polish letters, language, and history. He embarked on this project, which would probably have resulted in a university career, before the Nazi occupation of Poland. He gave special attention to the interplay of word and deed in the history of Poland and, later, to the interplay between word and deed in biblical history. In his own early poetic and dramatic works, his fascination with the word, whether spoken in conversation or written in parts declaimed on a stage, created what was called the "theater of the living word."

With other students who met secretly when their university was closed by the Nazi occupiers, he formed what was called the Rhapsodic Theater Company. In occupied Poland, this meant a theater company that wrote and produced plays with no resources — no scenery, no costumes — apart from the living word itself. In this theater of the inner self, the action arises out of the meaning of words and the problems they articulate rather than through the impact of event upon character, as is the case in ordinary theater. Wojtyła explained, "The supremacy of word over gesture indirectly restores the supremacy of thought over movement and impulse in man."[4]

His third play, *Our God's Brother*, is a case in point in his use of words. Wojtyła is not a poet who grabs you with beautiful language that evokes images of things. His is imagery born of action but, in this play, there are many voices talking — internal voices and external voices — no action, just voices talking to one another. In the

4. Karol Józef Wojtyła, "Drama of Word and Gesture," in *The Collected Plays and Writings in Theater* (Berkeley: University of California Press, 1987), 380.

conversation, however, one sees something develop that discloses Wojtyła's inner life.

When Karol Wojtyła was elected pope, I asked a Polish priest in Rome, "What was he known for as a bishop? What did he do?" He responded not by speaking of what Cardinal Wojtyła had done but with the observation, "What he was most known for was carefully selecting always the exact word to fit the occasion." I didn't understand this response very well until I started to look at the new pope's intellectual background and his scholarly training.

Our God's Brother is a study of an actual Pole (his real name was Albert Chmielowski, who is now a canonized saint, but Wojtyła used the name "Adam" in the play). He was born in 1845, and as a young man he was involved in insurrection against Poland's Russian occupiers at the time. He became an artist, a painter. He experienced a religious conversion and adopted a form of religious life, the Franciscan rule, and lived in Krakow. One of the particularities about the order he started, both for men and women, is that they don't just serve the poor and then have their own community life; they have to live with the poor. Chmielowski died among the poor in 1916, and Karol Wojtyła named him "Our God's Brother."

In this play, the major topic of conversation, the subject in which the word lives, is the social responsibility of art. This is a play written by an artist for a group of artists at a time when Poland was occupied by a foreign power, when Poles could not exercise social responsibility in ordinary ways. Was there, in this situation, a special role for Polish artists? The play's conversation about art and society is carried by several voices external to Adam himself. A colleague of Adam protests against subjectivism in art because it betrays the true nature of artistic creation. "For," the colleague protests, "in reality something slowly grows around you (during the process of artistic creation), gathers momentum, widens. Of course, though you have a part in it, you are not the only originator of this mystery."[5] Art is not subjective self-expression so much as the expression of something that the artist serves, although a few elements of subjective self-expression or of Feuerbach's theological approach can be used to interpret the Second Vatican Council. Some of the circle of voices in the play therefore consider Adam to be a seeker who is drawn out of himself, out of his own subjective, though artistic, creation. Adam himself, however, remains unconvinced by this argument against subjectivism because he sees his own painting as a means of his own subjective project, even of running away from something or from someone that is still indefinable for him. Adam uses self-expression for a personal purpose, a subjective purpose: escape.

Then another painter friend (another voice called

5. Ibid., 163.

Max) does just the opposite; he defends subjectivism in art, arguing that it is sufficient that an artist explore his own selfhood and give it expression. Whether or not it interests others is beside the point. This colleague admits that he has a public persona, but he dubs this public persona "the exchangeable man," — the commercial man, subject to the barter of social life.[6] A genuine and inviolable person, he insists, is private, a non-exchangeable man, withdrawn behind the fortress façade of inaccessible loneliness. But another voice, that of an artist, protests that such pure subjectivism diminishes the meaning of art and its creative power; and so the discussion goes on, passed from voice to voice.

It's a very philosophical play, as are all Wojtyła's plays and poetry. Adam/Albert cannot accept, on the one hand, the isolated loneliness advocated by his colleague Max. But neither can he be satisfied with the safe routine of social life. He says in the play, "Yes, we are hiding; we escape to little islands of luxury, to the so-called social life, to so-called social structure, and we feel secure. But, no, this security is a big lie — it's an illusion. It blinds our eyes and stops up our ears, but it will shatter in the end."[7]

This is the manner in which the pope explored ideas not only in plays but also in his encyclicals. He was a man of dialogue. He's creating all the voices in

6. Ibid., 164.
7. Ibid., 179.

the play, but they are genuinely different voices. One of them is called "the Stranger," without any personal name. He represents the revolutionary who counts on the anger of the poor to break open the circle of poverty in the name of justice denied. Nowhere does Adam, the protagonist, deny the truth of what this stranger is representing in the conversation; but it's not for Adam. Adam/Albert rebukes the stranger for exploiting the just anger of the poor. Here is a man who was an artist who also lived with the poor; he knew their anger and he recognizes the justice of that anger. Persisting under anger, however, and in the name of an at-this-point-unnamed love, that indefinable something that keeps calling Albert out of himself, Albert calls upon the poor to "Be one of us!"[8] He also asks the poor to acknowledge a wider and deeper poverty that lies beyond the mere lack of material goods. This is the poverty of values, for human beings are meant to aspire to all goods, to the "whole vastness of the values to which man is called," as Wojtyła writes.[9] And the greatest good calls not for anger but for love.

Besides all these external voices in the play, there are a number of inner voices. The reader is never sure in this dramatic inner space whether these voices are speaking for the protagonist, for Adam, or not. There's an inner

8. Ibid., 237.
9. Ibid., 243.

voice, in fact, that's dubbed "the Other." The Other seems to represent in some way the mind of the Enlightenment intelligentsia, of that division between theocentrism and anthropocentrism that Wojtyła wished to overcome. The Other calls upon the Adam/Albert within himself, because every modern intellectual has that interior conversation. The Other calls Adam to human maturity. Adam, however, finds it a call to a truncated maturity, because it rests everything upon merely understanding the world as it is, without shouldering the world's burdens — in other words, the Other speaks for a disengaged intellectualism.

At this point, Adam/Albert finds his own salvation through action whereby he helps a poor man whom he notices leaning against a lamppost in the cold, dark street. Recall the episode in Francis of Assisi's life where he met the leprous beggar, shared his clothing with him, and kissed him. The action of that kiss was the moment when Francis turned to God. Here again we find a conversation shaped by philosophical images that, at a certain point, are broken open by an action that reveals a deeper image, not an imaginative picture in the ordinary way that we would look for it. In this poor man, instead, Adam comes at last to see an image. It's not an easy vision, however, and he struggles against the awareness that he must give himself up to it generously if he is to identify with it. He cries out, "How can I cease to be who I am?"[10] Nevertheless, it is through this self-shattering discovery of the poor man that Adam is able to say, "I am not alone."[11] That's exactly what it means to be a theocentric humanist. One is never alone, not even in the privacy of one's study, or in the privacy of one's thoughts. "I am not alone."

The newly discovered "image" is not, however, a visual image to which art gives expression. It's not that visual art doesn't count; in the play, Adam's priest confessor tells him that his painting is religiously very important. God reveals himself to others through human creativity, and the confessor tells Adam, "God regards your art with a loving father's eye."[12] But Adam has seen a deeper image than visual art alone can shape: a nonpictorial image, "imperceptible," he says, "to my eye, but that preys upon my soul, my inner self."[13] This is an intimation of John Paul's work as a phenomenologist, for a phenomenologist is a philosopher of the interior life — necessarily connected, however, to external visible action.

It is finally clear that it is the very image of God that is struggling for recognition in all these living voices; these living words come to realization first of all in Adam's own soul and in that of the poor man. Calling out to the Other, the voice of Enlightenment, Adam shouts with joy over having given up "the tyranny of intelli-

10. Ibid., 207.   11. Ibid., 185.
12. Ibid., 208.   13. Ibid., 204.

gence" — that is, of an intelligence without love, with "[a too clear] image of the world," a conceptual image alone.[14] Instead Adam has found a different, deeper mysterious image. The Other does not or cannot understand him; the Enlightenment voice must fail to understand him. Adam expresses a liberation beyond Enlightenment: "You don't know! There is a sphere in my thought that you do not possess, you conceptualist, you Enlightenment philosopher."[15] Exposed here is an incompleteness of the Enlightenment project and, in a sense, the justification for the path that Karol Wojtyła himself took — to give up art and poetry for another vocation, and yet not to abandon his first reaction but to subsume it into something higher, more complete.

Wojtyła's sense of the relationship between word and deed furnishes a number of metaphors and images for God that depart from the more traditional vocabulary he used in his teaching as pope. If one goes to the encyclicals and the official teaching, you will find him talking about God the Father as Law Giver, Creator, Judge. You will find him speaking about the second Person of the Trinity as Redeemer, Man of Sorrows, Lamb of God, Master, Good Shepherd, Teacher, King, Spouse, Head — all biblical images, all necessary to the tradition. The third Person of the Trinity, the Holy Spirit, is called

14. Ibid., 222.
15. Ibid., 205.

Counselor, the Breath of Divine Love, the Giver of Gifts, Spirit, Love itself. These are marvelous images, but they are not Karol Wojtyła's. They don't give us insight into his original inner culture, his unique imagination.

Looking at Wojtyła's first play, which was called *Job, the Sufferer*, written shortly after the Nazis took over Poland, one finds God compared to the values that appear also in *Our God's Brother*. God is compared to harmony, to truth, to beauty and, in one line, God is "the bright one who brings light."[16] These images of light can take one by surprise when going through Wojtyła's poetry. Light is an image that permeates all his early writings. In a poem called "The Shores of Silence," line 26 says "the element of light, brightness breathes from every side, your Friend, a single spark, yet Luminosity itself.... Like a light filled with green, like green with no shade, an ineffable green that rests on drops of blood."[17]

The poem that he called "Looking into the Well at Sichar" presents a series of juxtapositions of words without many verbs. One must sit back and allow the words to work on one's inner soul. Wojtyła coins a phrase that returns in other poems: "Multitudes tremble in you transfixed by the light of your words as by the brightness of water." Water so bright, and lightness itself, come back again and again; they're joined together in

16. Ibid., 68.

17. Jerzy Peterkiewicz, trans., *Karol Wojtyła: Poems* (Krakow: Wydawnictwo, 1998), 10–12.

this phrase "the brightness of water." In a poem "Later Recollection of a Meeting," he speaks about one participant he had met: "He was a great gathering of perception like the well blowing brightness of water into a face. He had a mirror like the well — shining deep in the brightness of water."[18] And in a poem with that title, "The Song of the Brightness of Water," Wojtyła talks again about brightness like a mirror in the well.[19] In another poem, he puts himself into both the voice and the persona of a woman looking in wonder and astonishment at her only child. The poem is called, "Her Amazement at Her Only Child," and Wojtyła reflects, "The light that lingered in ordinary things like a spark sheltered under the skin of our days, the light was you.... you as the fruit of my body, my blood."[20]

The choice to use light as the primary verbal illumination for God's presence focuses the question about Wojtyła's inner culture: his own sense of a particular inner light. Striking evidence of that inner light is his contribution to the devotion of the rosary. Following on the issuance in 2002 of his apostolic letter *Rosarium Virginis Mariae*, the Church now has five luminous mysteries, mysteries of light, in that believers look at Christ and see him for what he is: the *Lumen gentium*, the light of the nations.

18. Ibid., 46   19. Ibid., 58.
20. Ibid., 66.

Of the various dimensions of the late Pope St. John Paul's inner life, and therefore of his life with a humanistic God here on earth, two are of particular importance. He was a phenomenologist philosophically and he was a mystic spiritually. A phenomenologist is a philosopher who walks around mental phenomena in order to see them. He is someone who looks at the phenomenon piece by piece in order to see things whole. But the phenomena appear in consciousness, and the phenomenologist is a philosopher of consciousness who carefully tracks the way objects come to appear in human consciousness. In *Person and Act (The Acting Person)*,[21] his basic philosophical work, Wojtyła worked to put together an objective metaphysical structure of personality with a phenomenological exploration of human consciousness. He brought us to look at consciousness itself, going beyond the object seen to reflection, where the ego looking becomes object to itself (I look at myself looking at this object) and finally to a reflexive process, as he calls it, where subjective consciousness becomes aware of itself subjectively as the source of light for knowing whatever is to be known, the looking itself as an inner activity, the human *a priori*, if it can be expressed in that manner. In some way, one can

21. Wojtyła, *The Acting Person* [*Osoba i Czyn*], trans. Andrzej Potocki and Anna-Teresa Tymieniecka, *Analecta Husserliana 10* (Boston: D. Reidel, 1979).

trace this consideration back to the Kantian intellectual *a priori*; one can even trace it back to Aristotle's agent intellect. If there isn't an intellectual agent in the act of knowing, there can't be any known object. But the way Wojtyła traces this development and correlation between object and subject, this subjective pursuit of subjective consciousness leading him back to this inner light, is original and would not have been possible without his study, first of neo-Scholastic philosophy, and second, of contemporary phenomenology. Whether or not he brought these together successfully is going to be an object of academic discussion for a long time. The controversy has not been helped by the translator of his great work, *The Acting Person*, who is determined, since she herself is a great phenomenologist, to prove Wojtyła a phenomenologist, that is, a philosopher who studies human consciousness from a first-person point of view. If you read the book only in its English translation, you will see that much that derives from neo-Scholastic terminology has been taken out and what is given is a translation that over-psychologizes Wojtyła's phenomenology. When one picks up the original Polish, by contrast, one sees the Latin tags that reflect Wojtyła's neo-Scholastic formation, the ontological skeleton on which the future pope hangs his phenomenological exercise.

For Wojtyła, consciousness is not ultimate; he was

not a philosophical idealist. The consciousness analyzed is always that of the human subject who is a human being. In the analysis of being, Thomistic metaphysical vocabulary comes into play. In *The Acting Person*, however, Wojtyła tells us that reflecting consciousness penetrates and illuminates whatever becomes in any way man's cognitive possession. This literally puts in mind, or into mind, what classical philosophy has called immanence, that interior light that belongs to what we would call consciousness as such, the proper sphere of its activity by which the mind appropriates its received contents according to its own immaterial mode.

Here perhaps Wojtyła is more Augustinian than he is Thomistic. He works out of the Platonic-Augustinian tradition of the metaphysics of light. He puts this tradition into contemporary phenomenological discourse. Wojtyła remarks that consciousness not only reflects but also interiorizes, in its own specific manner, what it mirrors, thus enclosing or capturing it in the person's ego. In mirroring the immanent content served up to cognitive activity, consciousness reaches a certain awareness, although this illumination is not the same as cognitive objectification. Rather, it is the return to the self and the self's inner light that makes possible knowing anything at all precisely as a human knower. Here are the beginnings of a phenomenological description of consciousness as spirit, even though the full reality of spirit is not completely accessible to such a phenomenological description. Nevertheless, it is a description that can be drawn from the experience of our own moral causality. Unlike Husserl and other phenomenologists, Wojtyła was not reflecting on the act of knowing as such, he was not an idealist. He was reflecting on what we discover about ourselves in our action and in knowing our action. It's not a reflection upon our ideas as such. It's a bringing to full self-consciousness the actions that connect us through our own generosity to a world that gives itself to those who love it.

Wojtyła was a phenomenologist who is a mystic; this is the second dimension of John Paul's inner culture that needs to be highlighted. Wojtyła's doctoral dissertation in theology was written on the act of faith according to the Carmelite mystic John of the Cross, the act of faith being the most interior way of looking at the objective contents of the apostolic deposit of the faith. He wrote his dissertation in Rome at a time when scholastic terminology and methodology were the *lingua franca* of the ecclesiastical faculties. His director was the great Dominican Thomist, Reginald Garrigou-Lagrange, who analyzed even the poet St. John of the Cross in Scholastic terms, and that's what Wojtyła had to do, too. Furthermore, Wojtyła wrote his dissertation in Latin, a language good for law and for scholastic methodology, but not well adapted for doing the kind of concrete psychological analysis that phenomenology uses. His use of phenomenological tools for analyzing the self-awareness that arises in acting was postponed until his postdoctoral thesis on Max Scheler, a philosopher who explored the phenomenology of the emotions.

The content of Wojtyła's contemplation as a mystic was, of course, faith and its mysteries. As pope, he explored the deposit of faith from various angles in weekly audiences, in encyclicals, and discourses. He assimilated the objective content of the faith in his own person at the deepest level of subjectivity.

His was a contemplative life. In 2002, I had the privilege of preaching the pope's annual retreat. He was an attentive listener, but he was attentive most of all to God rather than to anything a retreat master might say. He began his day with an hour of contemplation before celebrating the Eucharist; he recited the Liturgy of the Hours; he prayed the rosary and other devotions throughout the day. Constantly, he was in touch with the Lord. The result of this outer and inner life of prayer was a mystic's conviction that God is in all things and that all things can be seen through a divine prism, that God is a source of light and action with whom we're called to cooperate by our own seeing, our own cognition, and our own action, to cooperate rather than to combat. God is not jealous of our activity; nor should we be jealous of how God encourages and blesses it, for it shows how we are made in the image of a God who acts to create us, to save us, and make us saints. Out of this mystic's conviction has come the deep courage that was seen in his pastoral initiatives and actions throughout his papacy.

Pope John Paul II then, from the beginning of his pontificate, set out to enable us to see things whole and to be aware of how our self-consciousness is to be universal in intention and in action, in our missionary activity, and in God's making us holy day by day. He would say that we should see things whole by recognizing God in his creation, especially in the inner dynamics of human persons made in God's image and likeness. We should see the working of God in human history. His final poetic work, *Roman Triptych*, was a collection of three poems comprising a meditation that has the pope in contemplation before Michelangelo's great frescoes in the Sistine Chapel.[22] There he sees a reprise of salvation history from the creation of the world to the Last Judgment, and the result of a kind of artistic contemplation on the part of Michelangelo himself. He envisions the conclave that will follow his death and he is filled with concern for the legacy of the keys, not his personal subjective legacy, but the authority of Peter, given him by Christ and continued in the ministry of Peter's successor, the Bishop of Rome. In these poems it

22. John Paul II, *Roman Triptych Meditations* (Washington, D.C.: United States Conference of Catholic Bishops, 2003).

is Wojtyła's prayer that those who will elect his successor should see themselves in the midst of the beginning and the end, between the day of creation and the day of judgment, and that out of this may come, he prays, transparency and light, the clarity of events, and the clarity of consciousness. They shall find that the images of God he has pointed up throw light on who they are, on their beginning and on their end, on the place of their encounter with the Eternal Word and thus their encounter with the ground of a spirituality for the future, a spirituality that advances the conversation between faith and reason, both personally and publicly.

Bibliography

Abbott, Walter M., ed. *The Documents of Vatican II*. New York: Guild Press, 1966.

Aquinas, Thomas. *Lectura super Evangelium S. Ioannis*. Rome: Marietti, 1952.

Augustine. *The First Catechetical Instruction [De catechizandis rudibus]*. Translated by Rev. Joseph P. Christopher. Westminster, Md.: Newman Bookshop, 1946.

———. *The City of God*. Translated by Henry Bettensen. Harmondsworth: Penguin, 1972.

———. *The Works of St. Augustine: A Translation for the 21st Century*. Part 3, *Sermons*. Vol. 3, *Sermons 51–94*. Translated by Edmund Hill. Brooklyn, N.Y.: New City Press, 1991.

———. *The Works of St. Augustine: A Translation for the 21st Century*. Part 3, *Sermons*. Vol. 10, *Sermons 341–400*. Translated by Edmund Hill, OP. Hyde Park, N.Y.: New City Press, 1995.

———. *Teaching Christianity [De doctrina christiana]*. Translated by Edmund Hill, OP. Hyde Park, N.Y.: New City Press, 1996.

———. Augustine. *The Works of St. Augustine: A Translation for the 21st Century*. Part 1, *Books*. Vol. 1, *The Confessions*. Translated by Maria Boulding, OSB. Hyde Park, N.Y.: New City Press, 1997.

———. *The Augustine Catechism: The Enchiridion on Faith, Hope and Love*. Translated by Bruce Harbert. Hyde Park, N.Y.: New City Press, 1999.

———. *Expositions of the Psalms: 51–72*. Translated by Maria Boulding, OSB. Hyde Park, N.Y.: New City Press, 2001.

Benedict XVI. "Address to the Roman Curia Offering them his Chrismas Greetings." September 2005. *The Holy See*, http://w2.vatican.va/content/benedict-xvi/en/speeches/2005/december/documents/hf_ben_xvi_spe_20051222_roman-curia.html.

———. "Faith, Reason, and the University: Memories and Reflections." Lecture at Regensburg University. September, 12, 2006. *The Holy See*, http://w2.vatican.va/content/benedict-xvi/en/speeches/2006/september/documents/hf_ben-xvi_spe_20060912_university-regensburg.html.

Bonner, Gerald. "Augustine's Understanding of the Church as a Eucharistic Community." In *Saint Augustine the Bishop: A Book of Essays*, edited by Fannie LeMoine and Christopher Kleinhenz, 39–63. New York: Garland, 1994.

Burtchaell, James Tunstead, CSC.*The Dying of the Light*. Grand Rapids, Mich.: Wm. E. Eerdmans, 1998.

Congregation for the Doctrine of the Faith, *Mysterium ecclesiae*. June 24, 1973.

———. *Dominus Jesus*. Rome: Typis Polyglottis Vaticanis, 2000.

De Lubac, Henri. *Catholicism: Christ and the Common Destiny of Mankind*. Foreword by Joseph Cardinal Ratzinger. Translated by Lancelot C. Sheppard and Sister Elizabeth England, OCD. San Francisco: Ignatius Press, 1988.

Dulles, Avery. *The Catholicity of the Church*. Oxford: Oxford University Press, 1985.

Dworkin, Ronald, et al. "Assisted Suicide: The Philosophers' Brief." *New York Review of Books*, March 27 1997. http://www.nybooks.com/articles/archives/1997/mar/27/assisted-suicide-the-philosophers-brief/.

Evans, Gillian R. "Augustine and the Church." In *Saint Augustine the Bishop: A Book of Essays*, edited by Fannie LeMoine and Christopher Kleinhenz, 167–74. New York: Garland, 1994.

Gleason, Philip. *Contending with Modernity: Catholic Higher*

Education in the Twentieth Century. New York: Oxford University Press, 1995.

Grabownski, Stanislaus J. *The Church: An Introduction to the Theology of St. Augustine*. St. Louis: Herder, 1957.

Graff, Gerald. *Beyond the Culture Wars: How Teaching the Conflicts Can Revitalize American Education*. New York: W. W. Norton, 1992.

Israel, Jonathan. *The Radical Enlightenment: Philosophy and the Making of Modernity (1650–1750)*. Oxford: Oxford University Press, 2001.

John Paul II. *Redemptor hominis*. Rome: Typis Polyglottis Vaticanis, 1979.

———. *Dives in misericordia*. Rome: Typis Polyglottis Vaticanis, 1980.

———. *Ut unum sint*. Rome: Typis Polyglottis Vaticanis, 1995.

———. *Roman Triptych Meditations*. Washington, D.C.: United States Conference of Catholic Bishops, 2003.

Kevane, Eugene. *Augustine the Educator: A Study in the Fundamentals of Christian Formation*. Westminster, Md.: Newman Press, 1964.

Lamb, Matthew. "Vatican II after Fifty Years: The Virtual Council versus the Real Council." In *The Second Vatican Council: Celebrating Its Achievements and the Future*, edited by Gavin D'Costa and Emma Jane Harris, 7–18. London: A. and C. Black, 2014.

Lindbeck, George. *The Nature of Doctrine: Religion and Theology in a Postliberal Age*. Philadelphia: Westminster, 1984.

MacIntyre, Alastair. *After Virtue: A Study in Moral Theory*. 3d. ed. Notre Dame, Ind.: University of Notre Dame Press, 2007. First edition published by Gerald Duckworth, London, 1981, and first U.S. edition, University of Notre Dame Press, 1981.

Marion, Jean-Luc. *God Without Being*. Chicago: University of Chicago Press, 1991.

Marrou, Henri S. *Agostino e la fine della cultura antica*. Milan: Jaca, 1987.

Marsden, George M. *The Soul of the American University: From Protestant Establishment to Established Nonbelief*. New York: Oxford University Press, 1994.

———. *The Outrageous Idea of Christian Scholarship*. Oxford: Oxford University Press, 1997.

Milbank, John. *Theology and Social Theory*. Oxford: Blackwell, 1992.

Newman, John Henry. *Apologia pro vita sua*. New York: Longmans, 1908.

———. *An Essay on the Development of Christian Doctrine*. London: Basil Montagu Pickering, 1878.

O'Malley, John W., SJ. *What Happened at Vatican II?* Cambridge, Mass.: Harvard University Press, 2010.

Paul VI. "Address During the Last General Meeting of the Second Vatican Council." 1965. *The Holy See*, http://w2 .vatican.va/content/paul-vi/en/speeches/1965/documents/ hf_p-vi_spe_19651207_epilogo-concilio.html.

Pelikan, Jaroslav. *The Christian Tradition: A History of the Development of Doctrine*. Vol. 5. Chicago: University of Chicago Press, 1991.

Peterkiewicz, Jerzy, trans. *Karol Wojtyła: Poems*. Krakow: Wydawnictwo, 1998.

Przywara, Erich, SJ. *An Augustine Synthesis*. New York: Sheed and Ward, 1936.

Ratzinger, Joseph. "Primacy, Episcopate and Apostolic Succession." In *The Episcopate and the Primacy*, by Karl Rahner and Joseph Ratzinger, 37–63. New York: Herder and Herder, 1962.

———. *A New Song for the Lord: Faith in Christ and Liturgy*. New York: Crossroad Herder, 1997.

Redfield, Robert. *The Folk Culture of the Yucatan*. Chicago: University of Chicago Press, 1941.

Roberts, Alexander, James Donaldson, and A. Cleveland Coxe, eds. *The Ante-Nicene Fathers*. Vol. 1. Grand Rapids, Mich.: W. B. Eerdmans, 1981.

Royal, Robert. *The God That Did Not Fail: How Religion Built and Sustains the West*. New York: Encounter, 2006.

Spadero, Antonio. "A Big Heart Open to God: The Exclusive Interview with Pope Francis." *America*, September 30, 2013; http://americamagazine.org/pope-interview.

Spinoza, Benedict de. *A Theologico-Political Treatise; A Political Treatise*. Mineola, N.Y.: Dover, 2004.

Tanner, Kathryn. *Theories of Culture: A New Agenda for Theology*. Minneapolis: Fortress, 1997.

Tracy, David. *The Analogical Imagination: Christian Theology and the Culture of Pluralism*. New York: Crossroad, 1998.

Vatican II. *Dignitatis humanae* [Decree on Religious Freedom]. In Abbott, *The Documents of Vatican II*, 1966, 675–96.

———. *Gaudium et Spes*. In Abbott, *The Documents of Vatican II*, 1966, 249–58.

———. *Nostra aetate*. "Declaration on the Relationship of the Church to Non-Christian Religions." In Abbott, *The Documents of Vatican II*, 1966, 660–68.

———. *Unitatis redintegratio* [Decree on Ecumenism]. In Abbott, *The Documents of Vatican II*, 1966, 341–66.

Von Balthasar, Hans Urs. *The Moment of Christian Witness*. San Francisco: Ignatius Press, 1969.

———. *The Glory of the Lord,* Vol. 7. San Francisco: Ignatius Press, 1969.

———. *Paul Struggles with His Congregation*. San Francisco: Ignatius Press, 1992.

———. *Explorations in Theology*, Vol. 4. San Francisco: Ignatius Press, 1995.

Wilken, Robert Louis. *The Spirit of Early Christian Thought: Seeking the Face of God*. New Haven: Yale University Press, 2003.

———. "Catholic Scholars, Secular Schools." *First Things* 179 (January 2008): 40–43.

Wojtyła, Karol Józef. "Drama of Word and Gesture." In *The Collected Plays and Writings in Theater*. Berkeley: University of California Press, 1987, 380–82.

Index

Acting Person, The (Wojtyła), 174, 186–88
Ad salutem humani generis (Pius XI), 43
Aeterni Patris (Leo XIII), 109
Albert the Great, Saint, 76–78, 82
Ambrose, Saint, 9
analytic philosophy, 112–13
angels, 170
apostolicity: "adequately express" divine realities, 69–70; Aquinas on, 56–60; cultural problems, 74–75; discipleship, 50–51; the Eucharist and sacramental worship, 56–62; Irenaus on, 50; the Magisterium and, 62–74; Peter as spokesman, 71–72; sacred texts and, 53; self-dispossession and, 68–69; as spiritual endowment, 70–71; textual scholarship, faith and, 53–56, 61–62; theology of, 50–62; tradition, as carrier of, 46–49; witness, obligation to bear, 51–53
applied ethics, 102, 111–15, 118–19, 121, 123
Aquinas, Saint Thomas: apostolicity, 56–60; Augustinian boldness, departure from, 90; being, concept of, 169; in the Catholic intellectual tradition, 9; the Eucharist, 56–60, 157; existentialist elements in, 17; faith, on the act of, 61n; *ipsum esse subsistens* (God as pure existence), 47; non-Christians, 15; Platonic-Augustinian-Aristotlelianism of, 12; reason and faith, 15, 81; *Summa contra gentiles,* 15; *Summa theologiae,* 57, 81; virtuous life, presentation of, 110
Aristotle, 16, 142
Augustine of Hippo, Saint: adversaries, 21, 23–25, 36–37; in the Catholic intellectual tradition, 9, 19–21, 40–44, 80; Christianity as rival to Rome, 90; *The City of God,* 29, 39–40, 90; *Commentary on Psalm 95,* 32–33; *Confessions,* 30; ecumenism and the unity of the Church, 27–40; existentialist elements in, 17; on heresy, 39n16; intellectual life, pursuit of, x–xi; monastic community formed by, 26–27; Platonism of, 12, 20, 22, 80; reason and faith, 15, 20–27; *Sermon 90,* 30–32; *Sermon 399,* 34–35; synthesis of philosophy and theology, 23; teaching as the essence of the apostolate, 42–43; *Teaching Christianity,* 42–43

Balthasar, Hans Urs von, 10, 15
Barth, Karl, 86

being: angels and the concept of, 170; univocal *vs.* analogical conceptions of, 169

Bellarmine, Robert, 10

Benedict of Nursia, Saint, 9, 78

Benedict XVI: Cardinal George, impact on, ix; faith and reason, connection between, 3–7; Peter as spokesman, 71; the pope as steward, 151; Second Vatican Council: hermeneutics of rupture and reform, 146–47, 149–50; Second Vatican Council: missionary Church, 164. *See also* Ratzinger, Joseph

Bible, the. *See* Holy Scripture

Bonaventure, Saint, ix

Bonner, Gerald, 36n12

Burtchaell, James, 103

catechesis, 156

Catherine of Siena, 9

Catholic Church: apostolicity as classical mark of, 46; Benedict XVI on, 164; catechesis, crisis in, 156; the Catholic intellectual tradition in, 13–17; common language creating culture, 143–44; ecclesial identity, path to loss of, 145–46; heavenly and visible, Augustine's distinction between, 40; heavenly and visible, distinction between, 35–36, 38; liturgy and devotion, rivalry between, 163; mission of, questions concerning, 160–62; pastoral and intellectual challenge of, 145; pastoral authority and governance, 155–56; pastoring following the Second Vatican Council, 163; theology of apostolicity, 50–62; theology of the Magisterium, 62–75; truth, tradition

as source of, 46–49; validity of the tradition, 159–60; the world and, relationship of, 151–52

Catholic health care institutions, 122

Catholic higher education: applied ethics, shift in, 111–22; barriers to reforming, 124–28; Catholic studies programs, 106–7; disjunction of the curriculum, 136; ethics, teaching of, 110–11; faculty hiring, 104–6; moral theology and philosophy, 108–11; religion in, 138; resources for reforming, 122–24; secularization, 104–8; truth and freedom, relationship of, 128

Catholic intellectual tradition: Augustine, influence of, 19, 40–44; in the Catholic Church, 13–17; Catholic scholars and, 95–96; doctrine of faith, translating the, 18–19; faith and reason, conversation between, 18–19; faith and reason, synthesis of, 1–2; freedom and truth, relationship between, 126; Greco-Roman culture and, 2–9; "handing on," 12–13; major figures, 9–10; spiritual life, 74; truth and, 9–13, 126; universities and, 9–11, 123

Catholic scholars: in the Catholic community, 97–98; description of, 79; as disciples of, 94–97; faith and reason, 82; goals, 81; historical development, 79–81; mission, 98–100; professional competence, 94; task in post-Christian society, 78–79; university context, 82–85. *See also* faith and world, distinction between

Catholic social teaching, 111, 124

Catholic way of life, 163

Chateaubriand, François-René de, 10

Chmielowski, Albert, 177

Christian phenomenology, 88–89

Christian religion: Catholic ; the early universities and, 9–10, 135; education and, 132; faith and, 130–31; improper de-Hellenization of, 4–5; spirituality and, 131–32; universities, importance of, 141; as a way of life, 49. *See also* Protestant/Protestantism

Christological doctrine/faith, 65–67

Church, the. *See* Catholic Church

Church and state, relationship of, 2

City of God, The (Augustine), 29, 39–40, 90

Commentary on Psalm 95 (Augustine), 32–33

Confessions (Augustine), 30

conversation between faith and culture, 45–49. *See also* faith and world, distinction between

conversation between faith and reason: Augustine's contribution, 20–27; Catholic scholars, 96–97; Christian religion and education, as relationship of, 132; common language for, 143–44; *credo ut intelligam* (I believe so that I can understand), 134–35; divine continuity in, 146; *fides quarens intellectum* (faith seeking understanding), 132–34; freedom as intrinsic to, 136; institutionalization of, 18, 45–46; John Paul II's contribution, 165, 192; multiple contexts for, 25–26; post-

Vatican II, 158–59; *saeculum*, taking place in, 45. *See also* faith and reason

correlational position, 85–86, 88

cultural pluralism, 5–6

culture: conversation between faith and, 45–49; faith as future carrier of, 142–43; Greco-Roman, 2–9; primacy of freedom in American, 137; problems of, 74–75; religion and education, relationship of, 137–38

Dante Alighieri, 15

Darwin, Charles, 102–3

Dawkins, Richard, 16

Dawson, Christopher, 89

Dennett, Daniel, 16

Dignitatis humanae (Second Vatican Council), 157

Dives in misericordia (John Paul II), 171

doctrinal accountability, 63

doctrinal language, abandonment of common, 153

Dominic, Saint, 9

Domininus Jesus (Congregation for the Doctrine of the Faith), 31–32

Donatists, 36–37

ecumenism, 27–40

education: Catholic universities; Christianity and, 132; critique by the faith community, failure of, 143; freedom in the dialogue between religion and, 136; legal instruction, 120; moral, 130; truth as purpose of, 12. *See also* Catholic higher education; conversation between faith and reason; universities

Emerson, Ralph Waldo, 95–96

empiricism, 76–77
Enlightenment, the, 166–67
Erasmus, 10
Eucharist, the: the apostolic
    mission and, 56–62, 66–67;
    Augustine on, 40; centrality of,
    161, 163
eugenics movement, 117
evangelizing, 153–54
Evans, Gillian R., 36n11, 37
evil, 161
Ex Corde ecclesiae (John Paul II),
    104–5
existentialism, 17

faith: in Christianity, 130–31; as
    critical, 133; culture, as future
    carrier of, 142–43; and culture,
    conversation between, 45–49;
    in the history of university
    disciplines, 140–41; mysteries
    of, 14–15; role of, 49; *saeculum*
    distinguished from, 77; textual
    scholarship and, 53–56; truth
    and, 21–22, 141–42
faith and reason: Benedict XVI on,
    3–7; for the Catholic scholar,
    82; Christian reason, 15–16;
    in contemporary secular uni-
    versities, 82–85; conversation
    between; de-Hellenization of
    Christianity, 5–6; the herme-
    neutic of reform, 152; Jewish
    modern orthodoxy, 81–82; rela-
    tionship of, 14–15; religion and
    science, antagonism between,
    6–7; in the secular university,
    84–85; separation in Western
    thought, 168; theology of apos-
    tolicity, 52–53; in the universal-
    ity of the Catholic intellectual
    tradition, 1–2; valuing of both
    by the Church, 13–14

faith and world, distinction
    between: Christian phenom-
    enology, 88–89; correlational
    position, 85–86, 88; neo-Augus-
    tinianism, 89–91; postliberal-
    ism, 87–88; secular/nonsecular,
    changing meaning of, 77–78;
    sociological dimension, 91–100;
    St. Albert's empiricism, 76–78;
    theological dimension, 78–91
Feuerbach, Ludwig, 174, 178
fideism, 24
Fides et ratio (John Paul II), 13, 84,
    168, 175
"Final Report of the Task Force on
    General Education" (Harvard
    University), 10–11
Francis, ix, xii, 158
Francis of Assisi, Saint, 9, 181
freedom: in the Catholic intel-
    lectual tradition, 16; cultural
    fault lines involving, 137; in the
    dialogue between religion and
    education, 136; faith as source
    of, 92; religious authority as
    threat to, 165–66; truth and, 75,
    126, 128
Frei, Hans, 87
French Revolution, 151–52
Friday abstinence from meat,
    152, 154
"fullness of time," 3

Gadamer, Hans-Georg, 86
Garrigou-Lagrange, Reginald, 189
Gaudium et spes (Second Vatican
    Council), 91, 125, 157
Gleason, Philip, 102–3, 122–24
Gnostics, 24–25
Graff, Gerald, 83
Greco-Roman culture, 2–9
Gutierrez, Gustavo, 90
Guzman, Saint Dominic, 9

Harnack, Adolf von, 5

Harris, Sam, 16

Harvard University: "Final Report
of the Task Force on General
Education," 10–12

Hegel, Georg Wilhelm Friedrich,
90

Heidegger, Martin, 85

"Her Amazement at Her Only
Child" (Wojtyła), 185

heresy, 39n16

hermeneutic of reform, 146,
151–52, 159–60

hermeneutic of rupture, 147, 149,
154–55, 160

holy orders, 61, 155, 157, 161

Holy Scripture: authority of, 28;
departures from, 79; divine
truth, as vehicle of, 69; faith, as
sole and sufficient rule of, 5; the
Magisterium, theological basis
for, 63–66, 167–68; method for
interpreting, 53–54, 61, 103;
Protestant schism over interpretation of, 103; read in the
liturgy, 61

horizon, notion of, xi–xii

Humanae salutis (John XXIII), 98

"I AM who am," 47

Ignatius of Loyola, 10

Incarnation, doctrine of, 66–67

individualism, 46, 74, 132, 162. See
also personal autonomy

Irenaeus, Saint, 50, 66, 73

Jerome, Saint, 9

Jesus Christ: the apostles and, 5,
50, 57, 59, 68–71; in Augustine's
thought, 23; authority of the
Magisterium from, 64–65, 72;
Catholic scholars as disciples of,
95–97, 100; the Church and, 74,
160–61; "Follow me," 50; as God
revealed, 23, 30, 49, 142; historical importance, 7; "I AM"
language, 47, 49; as mediator
between God and man, 58; the
"mind of Christ," 49; self-dispossession of, 68–69; Socrates,
similarities to, 7–9; time, existence outside, 49; truth and, 21,
75; uniqueness of, 30–32

Jewish modern orthodoxy, 81–82

Job, the Sufferer (Wojtyła), 184

John of the Cross, Saint, 10, 189

John Paul II: Acting Person, The
(Person and Act), 174; apostolic
teaching, maintaining and
reforming, 157; basic questions
listed by, 13; Cardinal George,
impact on, viii–ix; on the
Catholic university, 104; Christological foundation of Catholic
moral teaching, 67; Dives in
misericordia, 171; division of
concept and image, concern
to resolve, 166–67, 170–74; Ex
corde ecclesiae, 104–5; Fides et
ratio, 13, 84, 168, 175; godly
humanist in the writings of,
174–75; human and divine, linkage of, 171–73; humanist God,
"picture" of, 173–74; influence
of, 165–66; Mother Teresa and,
158; as mystic, 189–91; as phenomenologist, 182, 186–90; as
philosopher, 170; as poet, 167;
Redemptor hominis (The Redeemer of Mankind), 172; Redemptoris
missio, 173; on relativism, 84;
Roman Triptych, 191–92; Rosarium Virginis Mariae, 185; truth,
confidence in discovering, 142;
Ut unum sint, 173; words, use of,
177. See also Wojtyła, Karol

John XXIII, 41, 98, 100
Justin the Martyr, Saint, 9, 79–80, 82

Kant, Immanuel, 5
Khrushchev, Nikita, 101

"Later Recollection of a Meeting" (Wojtyła), 185
Lefebvre, Marcel François Marie Joseph, 156–57
legal instruction, 120
Leo X, 27
Leo XIII, 109
liberal Catholicism, 92–93
Lindbeck, George, 87–88
Lombard, Peter, 81
"Looking into the Well at Sichar" (Wojtyła), 184–85
de Lubac, Henri, 33–34
Lumen Christi Institute for Catholic Thought, 139
Lumen gentium (Second Vatican Council), 98, 125
Luther, Martin, 27

MacIntyre, Alasdair, 118, 121
Magisterium, the: authority of, Peter and, 72; Catholic university faculty and, 126–27; Christological basis, 66–67; eschatology of witness, 72–73; gifts of, cultural problems in receiving, 74–75; the Paschal mystery, 70; scriptural basis, 63–65, 67–68; teachings of Vatican II, dialogue with, vii–ix; theology of in the Church, 62–75; tradition, as carrier of, 46
Marion, Jean-Luc, 88–89
Maritain, Jacques, 10, 109
marriage, 161–62
Marsden, George, 103

Martyr, Saint Justin, 9, 79–80, 82
Marx, Karl, 90
Mies van der Rohe, Ludwig, 97
Milbank, John, 89–90
modernism, 1, 110
modernity, 22, 151–52
monastic institutions, 78
More, Thomas, 10
Mother Teresa of Calcutta, 158
mysteries of faith, 14–15

natural law, 67, 109, 144
neo-Augustinianism, 89–91
Newman, Cardinal John Henry, 10, 15, 42, 62–63, 68
Nicholas of Cusa, 9–10
Niebuhr, H. Richard, 90
Nietzsche, Friedrich, 142
Noll, Mark, 103
Nussbaum, Martha, 118

O'Malley, John, 149
Origen, 9
Our God's Brother (Wojtyła), 176–84

Pascal, Blaise, 10, 17
Paschal mystery, 70
pastoral authority, 155–56
pastoral governance, 150
Paul, Saint: in Athens, 12; as Catholic scholar, 79; Christological foundation of moral teaching, 67; on faith and reason, 3–4; the Gospel, urgency of preaching, 66; natural law, 144; on reason and faith, 15; "the mind of Christ," 49; on the uniqueness of Christ, 30–31
Paul VI, viii, 99, 158
Pelagians, 36
Pelikan, Jaroslav, 27–28
penance, 152–54, 161

personal autonomy, 74, 116, 127. *See also* individualism

Peter, Saint, 64–65, 67, 70–72, 191

Phaedo (Plato), 7–8

phenomenology: Christian, 88–89; of John Paul II, 182, 186–89; phenomenologist, description of, 186

philosophy: analytic, 112–13; applied ethics, 102, 111–15, 118–19, 121, 123; Augustinian, 22–23; the Catholic intellectual tradition and, 16–17; Christianity as, 80, 82; Enlightenment, 167; of John Paul II, 170, 187; moral, 102, 108–14, 118, 124; pragmatism, 129; reason in, 5–6

physician-assisted suicide, 115–17

Pius XI, 43

Plato, 7–8, 16

pluralism: Christological, 31; ideological in the university, 138; in moral theology, 109–10; religious, 75

political order, relationship of Church and, 2

popes, popular American conception of, 165–66

postliberalism, 87–88

progressivist societies, 48

Protestant/Protestantism: America as, 155; denominational schism over scriptural interpretation, 103; Reformation, 5; scholarship, 2; tradition as normative, rejection of, 46; universities, 9, 102–3

Ratzinger, Joseph: on apostolic succession and tradition, 51; in the Catholic intellectual tradition, 10; on the Church's place in theology, 56; on witnessing, 52. *See also* Benedict XVI

Rawls, John, 113–15, 118

reason: foundational principles, inability to establish, 117–19; limits of, 15–16, 133–34. *See also* faith and reason

Redemptor hominis (John Paul II), 172

Redemptoris missio (John Paul II), 173

Redfield, Robert, 153n

Reformation, the, 5

relativism, 84

religion: authentic, fears regarding, 74; freedom in the dialogue between education and, 136; individualism in, 162; legalistic American conception of, 165; as moral code, 129–30; *true vs. revealed,* 55. *See also* Christian religion

religious pluralism, 75

Rhapsodic Theater Company, 176

Ricoeur, Paul, 86

Roman Triptych (John Paul II), 191–92

Rosarium Virginis Mariae (John Paul II), 185

sacraments: apostles and apostolicity, 57, 60–61; holy orders, 61, 155, 157, 161; marriage, 161–62; penance, 152–54, 161; in touch with God through, 161–62; unnecessary in the presence of the Lord, 73. *See also* Eucharist the

sacred texts, 52–53, 81. *See also* Holy Scripture

saeculum, 41, 45, 77, 91

Scheler, Max, 190

Schliermacher, Friedrich, 85

Scotus, Duns, 169

scripture. *See* Holy Scripture

Second Vatican Council: anthropological turn of, 157–58; Catholic higher education, 123–24; change the world, call to, 145; Church's mission as anthropocentric and theocentric, 171; competing interpretations of, 148–49; conciliar texts of, 147–48; conversation between reason and faith, contribution to, 165; dialogical vision of, 143; *Dignitatis humanae*, 157; doctrinal development in teaching of, 156–57; *Gaudium et spes*, 91, 125, 157; healing a divided *saeculum*, 41–42, 91; hermeneutic of reform, 146, 151–52, 159–60; hermeneutic of rupture, 147, 149, 154–55, 160; impact of, xi; *Lumen gentium*, 98, 125; mission of the Church, 98; mysteries of faith, 159; natural law, 109; non-Catholics, relations with, 37–39; the papal Magisterium and, vii–ix; pastoral practice, changes in, 152–54; the pastoral question as reason for, 163–64; political interpretation of, 150–51; the *saeculum*, 41–42; subjective self-expression to interpret, 178; the uniqueness of Christ, 32

secularism, 77, 165–66

secularity, 77, 93

secularization: of Catholic universities, 104–8; of Protestant universities, 102–3

secular moral philosophy, 111–22

secular university, the: bringing religion into, 138–41; Christian responses to, 85–91; disciplinary specialization, 83–84; disjunction of the curriculum,

83–84, 135–36; faith and reason in, 82–85; faith in the history of various disciplines, 140–41; institutes of Catholic thought, 139–40

Sermon 90 (Augustine), 30–32

Sermon 399 (Augustine), 34–35

Sertillanges, Antonin-Gilbert, x

"Shores of Silence, The" (Wojtyła), 184

Simon, Yves, 109

Singer, Peter, 111–14

skeptics and skepticism, 21, 45

Socrates, 7–8, 11

"Song of the Brightness of Water, The" (Wojtyła), 185

Spinoza, Benedict de, 53–54

spirituality, 131–32, 192

St. Anselm Institute, 139

Stein, Edith, 10

Stoics, 21, 23

Suarez, Francisco, 168–69

Summa contra gentiles (Aquinas), 15

Summa theologiae (Aquinas), 57, 81

Tanner, Kathryn, 87–88

Teaching Christianity (Augustine), 42–43

Teresa of Avila, 10

Tertullian, 23–24

theology: of apostolicity, 50–62, 75; of Augustine, 19, 23; Catholic intellectual life and, 55; the Church, place in, 56; faith and reason, 81, 85–89; John Paul II and, 170, 189; liberal, 90; of Magisterium in the Church, 62–75; medieval, 90; methodological changes in Catholic moral, 108–11; moral, 102, 108–11, 122; philosophy and, synthesis of, 23

Therese of Lisieux, 10

Thomas, Saint. *See* Aquinas, Saint Thomas

Thomas à Kempis, 15

Tillich, Paul, 85

Tracy, David, 86–87

tradition: Catholicism *vs.* Protestantism regarding, 46; as source of religious truth, 46–49

tradition, the. *See* Catholic intellectual tradition

transcendence of God, 28–29, 93, 174

truth: Catholic intellectual tradition and, 11–13; confidence in discovering, 141–42; cultural fault line between freedom and, 137; faith and, 21–22, 141–42; of faith and reason, tension between, 45; freedom and, 126, 128; the Magisterium as the guarantor of, 62–63; religious claims of, fears regarding, 74–75; Socrates *vs.* Harvard regarding, 11; textual scholarship and, 53–56, 61–62; tradition as source of, 46–49; utilitarianism *vs.* wisdom, 55–56

uniqueness of Christ, 30–32

universities: creation of, 9–10, 134–35; criticism and creativity, misplaced valuing of, 10–11; research, departmentalization and, 135–36; secularization of Protestant, 102–3; state colleges, 9. *See also* Catholic higher education; secular university

Ut unum sint (John Paul II), 173

Vatican II. *See* Second Vatican Council

Wilken, Robert, 3, 139–40

witness, obligation to bear, 51–53

Wojtyła, Karol: *The Acting Person,* 174, 186–88; in the Catholic intellectual tradition, 10; "Her Amazement at Her Only Child," 185; images of God, use of, 168, 182–84; *Job, the Sufferer,* 184; "Later Recollection of a Meeting," 185; "Looking into the Well at Sichar," 184–85; *Our God's Brother,* 176–84; as philosopher, 170; "The Shores of Silence," 184; "The Song of the Brightness of Water," 185; words, use of, 175–77, 183–84. *See also* John Paul II

World Council of Churches, 85–86

Yale school, 87

Yeshiva University, 81–82